DISABILITY AND THE DISABLED-ISSUES, LAWS AND PROGRAMS

INDIVIDUALS WITH DISABILITIES EDUCATION ACT

DISPROPORTIONALITY ISSUES AND EARLY INTERVENTION SERVICES

DISABILITY AND THE DISABLED-ISSUES, LAWS AND PROGRAMS

Additional books in this series can be found on Nova's website under the Series tab.

Additional E-books in this series can be found on Nova's website under the E-book tab.

EDUCATION IN A COMPETITIVE AND GLOBALIZING WORLD

Additional books in this series can be found on Nova's website under the Series tab.

Additional E-books in this series can be found on Nova's website under the E-book tab.

DISABILITY AND THE DISABLED-ISSUES, LAWS AND PROGRAMS

INDIVIDUALS WITH DISABILITIES EDUCATION ACT

DISPROPORTIONALITY ISSUES AND EARLY INTERVENTION SERVICES

HAROLD SANDERS
EDITOR

New York

For permission to use material from this book please contact us:
Telephone 631-231-7269; Fax 631-231-8175
Web Site: http://www.novapublishers.com

LIBRARY OF CONGRESS CATALOGING-IN-PUBLICATION DATA

ISBN: 978-1-62808-180-0

Published by Nova Science Publishers, Inc. † New York

CONTENTS

oversight by the Department of Education and states. GAO analyzed data on early intervening services for school years 2009-10 and 2010-11; reviewed 16 states' methods for identifying districts required to provide services that included review of states that did and did not require districts to provide services; visited state educational agencies and school districts in 4 states; and interviewed Education and state officials.

Chapter 2 – The Individuals with Disabilities Education Act (IDEA) is both a grants statute and a civil rights statute. As a grants statute, IDEA provides federal funding for the education of children with disabilities and requires, as a condition for the receipt of such funds, the provision of a free appropriate public education (FAPE) (i.e., specially designed instruction provided at no cost to parents that meets the needs of a child with a disability). In FY2012, $12.6 billion was appropriated for IDEA. In the fall of 2009, 5.9 million children ages six through 21 received educational services under IDEA.

As a civil rights statute, IDEA contains procedural safeguards, which are provisions intended to protect the rights of parents and children with disabilities regarding the provision of FAPE. These procedures include parental rights to resolve disputes through a mediation process, and present and resolve complaints through a due process complaint procedure, and through state complaint procedures. IDEA's procedural safeguards also address disciplinary issues. In general, a child with a disability is not immune from discipline, but the procedures are not the same as for non-disabled children.

To be covered under IDEA, a child with a disability must meet the categorical definition of disability in the act, and the child must require special education and related services as a result of the disability in order to benefit from public education. Once a child meets IDEA's eligibility criteria, FAPE is implemented through the Individualized Education Program (IEP), which is the plan for providing special education and related services by the local educational agency (LEA). The IEP is developed by an IEP team composed of school personnel and parents. IDEA requires that children with disabilities be educated in the least restrictive environment. That is, to the maximum extent appropriate they are to be educated with children who are not disabled. In 2008, over 50% of all children with disabilities served by IDEA spent 80% or more of their time in a regular classroom.

To implement IDEA, states and other entities (i.e., the District of Columbia, Puerto Rico, the Bureau of Indian Education, the outlying areas, and the freely associated states) receive grants based on a statutory formula.

PREFACE

The overrepresentation of minority students in special education continues to be a persistent and challenging issue in education. This is a complicated issue because it is often difficult to determine if a student is struggling in school because of a disability or, as some suggest, other factors such as poverty, limited English proficiency, or factors within the school environment, such as a lack of high quality instruction or cultural bias. To illustrate, a 6th grade Hispanic girl who is not proficient in English may be diagnosed as having a learning disability because she is not reading at grade level. Similarly, an African American boy who may be acting out in school because of problems at home may be diagnosed as having an emotional disability. The consequences of overrepresentation have serious implications for students who may be inappropriately identified as having a disability because these students are placed in an educational track that is different than their peers which may negatively impact their academic and career outcomes. This book examines the disproportionality issues and early intervention services of the Individuals with Disabilities Education Act.

Chapter 1 – Concerned that certain racial and ethnic groups were overrepresented in special education, Congress in the 2004 reauthorization of IDEA required that school districts take certain actions to address this problem. Specifically, districts identified with "significant disproportionality' based on race and ethnicity must spend 15 percent of their IDEA funds t provide early intervening services to school age children who need addition academic and behavioral support. GAO was asked to review these ear intervening services. GAO examined (1) the numbers and characteristics districts that provide services and how states determine which districts required to provide services; (2) the types of services provided; and

Most of the federal funds received by states are passed on to LEAs based on a statutory formula. IDEA also contains state and local maintenance of effort (MOE) requirements and supplement, not supplant (SNS) requirements aimed at increasing overall educational spending, rather than substituting federal funds for education spending at the state and local levels.

Originally enacted in 1975, IDEA has been the subject of numerous reauthorizations to extend services and rights to children with disabilities. The most recent reauthorization of IDEA was P.L. 108-446 enacted in 2004. Funding for Part B, Assistance for Education of all Children with Disabilities, the largest and most often discussed part of the act, is permanently authorized. Funding for Part C, Infants and Toddlers with Disabilities, and Part D, National Activities, was authorized through FY2011. Funding for the programs continues to be authorized through annual appropriations.

Chapter 3 – The final regulations for the reauthorized Individuals with Disabilities Education Act (IDEA) were published in the Federal Register on August 14, 2006, and became effective on October 13, 2006. Since publication of the final regulations, the Office of Special Education and Rehabilitative Services (OSERS) in the U.S. Department of Education has received requests for clarification of some of these regulations. This is one in a series of question and answer documents prepared by OSERS to address some of the most important issues raised by requests for clarification on a variety of high-interest topics. Generally, the questions, and corresponding answers, presented in this Q&A document required interpretation of IDEA and the regulations and the answers are not simply a restatement of the statutory or regulatory requirements. The responses presented in this document generally are informal guidance representing the interpretation of the Department of the applicable statutory or regulatory requirements in the context of the specific facts presented and are not legally binding. The Q&As are not intended to be a replacement for careful study of IDEA and the regulations. The statute, regulations, and other important documents related to IDEA and the regulations are found at http://idea.ed.gov.

The final regulations incorporate new requirements regarding identifying children with specific learning disabilities (SLD) and early intervening services (EIS). With regard to identifying children with SLD, the regulations: (1) allow a local educational agency (LEA) to consider a child's response to scientific, research-based intervention as part of the SLD determination process; (2) allow States to use other alternative research-based procedures for determining whether a child has a SLD; (3) provide that States may not require the use of a severe discrepancy between intellectual ability and achievement to determine whether a child has a SLD; and (4) require a public agency to use the State criteria in determining whether a child has a SLD and discuss the role that response to scientific research-based interventions plays in a comprehensive evaluation process.

The regulations regarding EIS permit an LEA to use not more than 15% of its IDEA Part B funds to develop and implement EIS. The regulations also indicate how EIS funds can be expended; on whom the EIS funds can be spent; the reporting requirements for EIS; special provisions regarding disproportionality based on race and ethnicity and how that affects an LEA's use of EIS funds; and the relationship of EIS to maintenance of effort. The purpose of the questions and answers that follow is to provide additional guidance to States and LEAs in complying with the requirements regarding EIS and response to scientific research-based interventions to identify students with a SLD.

In: Individuals with Disabilities Education Act ISBN: 978-1-62808-180-0
Editor: Harold Sanders

Chapter 1

INDIVIDUALS WITH DISABILITIES EDUCATION ACT: STANDARDS NEEDED TO IMPROVE IDENTIFICATION OF RACIAL AND ETHNIC OVERREPRESENTATION IN SPECIAL EDUCATION*

United States Government Accountability Office

WHY GAO DID THIS STUDY

Concerned that certain racial and ethnic groups were overrepresented in special education, Congress in the 2004 reauthorization of IDEA required that school districts take certain actions to address this problem. Specifically, districts identified with "significant disproportionality" based on race and ethnicity must spend 15 percent of their IDEA funds to provide early intervening services to school age children who need additional academic and behavioral support. GAO was asked to review these early intervening services. GAO examined (1) the numbers and characteristics of districts that provide services and how states determine which districts are required to provide services; (2) the types of services provided; and (3) oversight by the Department of Education and states. GAO analyzed data on early intervening

---

* This is an edited, reformatted and augmented version of United States Government Accountability Office, Publication No. GAO-13-137, dated February 2013.

services for school years 2009-10 and 2010-11; reviewed 16 states' methods for identifying districts required to provide services that included review of states that did and did not require districts to provide services; visited state educational agencies and school districts in 4 states; and interviewed Education and state officials.

WHAT GAO RECOMMENDS

To promote consistency in determining which districts need to provide early intervening services, Education should develop a standard approach for defining significant disproportionality to be used by all states. Education proposed a revision to the recommendation, citing the need to collect more information. GAO continues to believe that the recommendation is valid as discussed in the report.

WHAT GAO FOUND

In 2010, states required about 2 percent of all districts to use Individuals with Disabilities Education Act (IDEA) funds for early intervening services to address the overrepresentation of racial and ethnic groups in special education. Based on definitions states individually developed to measure this overrepresentation— referred to in IDEA as significant disproportionality— 356 districts were required to provide services. Half of these districts were clustered in five states and 73 were in Louisiana alone. States have used flexibility provided by Education to develop their own definitions of significant disproportionality and GAO's analysis of 16 selected states found wide variation in definitions. Further, GAO found that the way some states defined overrepresentation made it unlikely that any districts would be identified and thus required to provide early intervening services. Nebraska and Louisiana illustrate differing outcomes that can result from different state definitions. In Nebraska, one of 21 states that did not require any districts to provide services in 2010-11, racial and ethnic groups must be identified for special education at a rate three times higher than for other groups for 2 consecutive years. In contrast, racial and ethnic groups in Louisiana districts must be identified for special education at twice the rate of other students in any year. GAO's analysis found if Nebraska had used Louisiana's definition,

Nebraska districts may have been required to provide services and, conversely, Louisiana might have identified fewer districts under Nebraska's definition.

Districts used their IDEA funds for a range of early intervening services including literacy and math tutoring as well as professional development to help educators address behavioral and emotional issues. For instance, one of the districts GAO visited provided struggling students with individualized math and reading instruction that resulted in improved performance.

Education's oversight of racial and ethnic groups' overrepresentation in special education is hampered by the flexibility states have to define significant disproportionality. Specifically, Education periodically reviews states' definitions as part of its onsite monitoring under IDEA, but the department has not required a state to change its definition when it makes it unlikely that overrepresentation will be identified. States in turn are required to identify districts and ensure that these districts reserve the required amount for early intervening services.

ABBREVIATIONS

IDEA	Individuals with Disabilities Education Act
Recovery Act	American Recovery and Reinvestment Act of 2009
OSEP	Office of Special Education Programs
OSERS	Office of Special Education and Rehabilitative Services
SY	School Year
RTI	Response to intervention

February 27, 2013
The Honorable Tom Harkin
Chairman
Committee on Health, Education,
Labor, and Pensions United States Senate

Dear Mr. Chairman:

The overrepresentation of minority students in special education continues to be a persistent and challenging issue in education. This is a complicated issue because it is often difficult to determine if a student is struggling in school because of a disability or—as some suggest—other factors such as poverty, limited English proficiency, or factors within the school environment, such as a lack of high quality instruction or cultural bias. To illustrate, a 6th grade Hispanic girl who is not proficient in English may be diagnosed as having a learning disability because she is not reading at grade level. Similarly, an African American boy who may be acting out in school because of problems at home may be diagnosed as having an emotional disability. The consequences of overrepresentation have serious implications for students who may be inappropriately identified as having a disability because these students are placed in an educational track that is different than their peers which may negatively impact their academic and career outcomes.

In response to concerns about overrepresentation of racial and ethnic groups in special education, the 2004 reauthorization of the Individuals with Disabilities Education Act (IDEA) included a provision allowing school districts the option of using up to 15 percent of their IDEA, Part B funds[1]—previously expended only for students with disabilities—to provide early intervening services[2] to students not currently receiving special education services but who need additional academic or behavioral supports to succeed in school. More significantly, the law requires a school district that is determined by its state as having "significant disproportionality"—a term not defined in law—to reserve 15 percent of its IDEA, Part B funds to provide early intervening services for students who are not currently in special education. You asked us to review issues related to these services. This report examines: (1) the numbers and characteristics of districts that provide early intervening services and how states determine which districts are required to provide these services, (2) the types of services provided, and (3) how the Department of Education (Education) and states oversee early intervening services.

To examine the numbers and characteristics of the districts that provided early intervening services, we analyzed Education's IDEA data for school years 2009-10 and 2010-11, which contained information on the number and characteristics of districts with students receiving special education and early intervening services provided,[3] IDEA, Part B child count data, and Education's Common Core of Data, which provided demographic data on all students in school districts. To assess the reliability of data from these data sets, we interviewed knowledgeable Education officials, reviewed documentation of data collection procedures, and conducted internal reliability checks. We determined that the data were sufficiently reliable for our purposes. To obtain more in depth information about early intervening services, we conducted site visits to eight districts in four states (California,

Florida, Maryland, and Texas) where we interviewed state and local officials, and visited schools that had provided early intervening services. We selected these states—which all required some districts to provide early intervening services in school year 2009-10— based on geography, the percentage of districts required to provide the services, and the percentage of districts that implemented the program voluntarily. Within those states, we selected districts that provided early intervening services based on location, whether they were required to implement the program or did so voluntarily, the amount they received in IDEA, Part B funding, poverty levels, and the percentage of students receiving special education services.

To identify how states determine which districts are required to provide early intervening services, we reviewed 16 states' methodologies for determining significant disproportionality. To ensure that our review of state methodologies included states that did and did not have districts identified as having significant disproportionality, we chose the six states with the highest percentage of districts required to provide services in school year 2009-10, and we randomly selected eight states that took into account the number of districts required to provide early intervening services, including 4 states that did not have any districts required to provide early intervening services. Further, we judgmentally selected two additional states due to the relatively low percentage of districts required to provide services. To identify the types of services that districts provided students, we reviewed data on services collected as part of Education's IDEA National Assessment Implementation Study, which collected information for school year 2008-09, and Education's early intervening services data. To examine how Education and states oversee the program, we reviewed relevant federal laws and regulations, Education's monitoring protocols, and the findings from Education's monitoring visits of the 16 states included in our review of significant disproportionality definitions. We also interviewed Education officials and state officials in the four states we visited about their monitoring efforts. See appendix I for more details on our scope and methodology.

We conducted this performance audit from January 2012 to February 2013 in accordance with generally accepted government auditing standards. Those standards require that we plan and perform the audit to obtain sufficient, appropriate evidence to provide a reasonable basis for our findings and conclusions based on our audit objectives. We believe that the evidence obtained provides a reasonable basis for our findings and conclusions based on our audit objectives.

BACKGROUND

Some groups of students are at greater risk of receiving special education than other students, and this trend has persisted over time (see fig. 1). Specifically, according to Education's data, African American and American Indian/Alaska Native students are at greater risk of receiving special education than students from other racial and ethnic groups.[4] Research suggests overrepresentation may be a consequence of several factors such as poverty, factors within the school environment, such as cultural bias, or some combination of these elements.

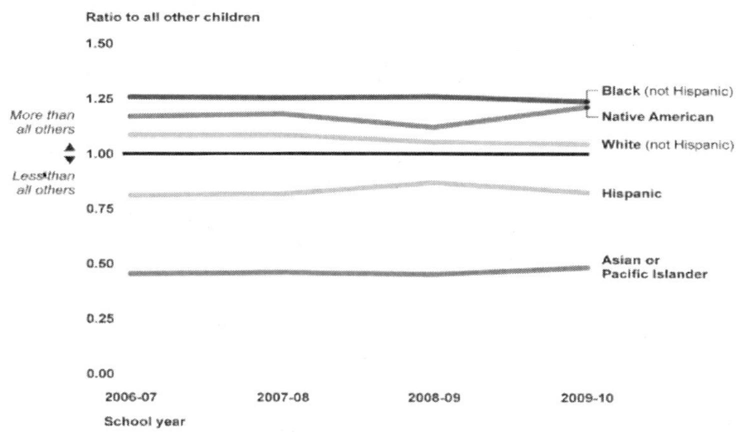

Source: Data presented at the 2012 IDEA Leadership Conference: Looking at Race/Ethnicity Disproportionality in Special Education from the Student Outcomes Side of the Educational System: Why Analyzing Disproportionality Matters for Results Improvement Planning. Data Accountability Center and Regional Resources Center Program, Washington, DC, 2012.

Notes: Risk ratio was defined as a specific racial or ethnic group's risk of receiving special education and related services divided by the risk for all other children. The data represent children ages 6 to 21. All school years, with the exception of school year 2009-10, are based on either 50 states (school years 2006-07 and 2008-09) or 49 states (school year 2007-8) reporting along with District of Columbia. School year 2009-10 is based on those 38 states and the District of Columbia that reported using the same 5 racial/ethnic categories used in the previous years. Beginning with school year 2010-11 and beyond, states are required to report using seven racial/ethnic categories.

Figure 1. Risk of Receiving Special Education, by Racial or Ethnic Group (School Years 2006-2010).

To address the issue of overrepresentation, in the last reauthorization of IDEA in 2004, Congress added provisions allowing school districts the option to use up to 15 percent of their Part B funding to provide early intervening services for students in kindergarten through grade 12 (putting particular emphasis on providing services to kindergarten through grade 3) who have not been identified as needing special education or related services, but who need additional academic and behavioral support to succeed in a general education environment. While the 2004 reauthorization of IDEA allowed districts the option to voluntarily provide early intervening services, it made it mandatory for districts with "significant disproportionality."[5] This term is used in the law to refer to the overrepresentation of racial and ethnic groups in special education, although it is not defined. Under IDEA, a school district is required to reserve 15 percent of its IDEA, Part B funds for early intervening services[6] if that district is found to have significant disproportionality in special education based on race and ethnicity with respect to: (1) the identification of children with disabilities; (2) the identification of children in particular disability categories; (3) the placement of children with disabilities in particular educational settings; and (4) the incidence, duration, and type of disciplinary actions, including suspensions and expulsions.

IDEA outlines two broad categories of activities for which districts may use funds for early intervening services: (1) professional development for teachers and other school staff, and (2) educational and behavioral evaluations, services, and supports, including scientifically-based literacy instruction. The law requires districts providing these services to report annually to the state on the number of students who received these services and the number of students served who subsequently receive special education and related services during the preceding 2-year period.[7]

Funding for early intervening services is authorized under Part B of IDEA. First enacted in 1975, IDEA is the primary federal law that addresses the educational needs of students with disabilities.[8] Under IDEA, Part B, Education provides grants to states that enable school districts to provide services to students with disabilities aged 3 through 21. In 2009, federal funding under IDEA, Part B was more than double the 2008 amount because of the American Recovery and Reinvestment Act of 2009 (Recovery Act) (see table 1). The Recovery Act provided districts additional funds that could be used for any allowable purposes under IDEA, including to retain teachers and other school personnel, purchase technological equipment such as computers, and provide teacher professional development, among other things.[9]

Table 1. IDEA, Part B Funding and Number of Children Served (Fiscal Years 2008- 2012)

Fiscal year	Federal funds (in billions)	Number of children with disabilities served aged 3-21 (in thousands)
2008	11.3	6,718
2009	23.6	6,599
2010	11.9	6,614
2011	11.9	6,558
2012	12.0	6,558

Source: Education's fiscal year 2013 budget request accessed on December 4, 2012 at: https://www2.ed.gov/about/overview/budget/budget13/justifications/index.html.

Until 2004, IDEA, Part B funds could only be used to provide services to children with disabilities. Currently, these funds can be used to provide early intervening services to students who have not been identified as needing special education services, but who need additional academic and behavioral support to succeed. IDEA is administered by Education's Office of Special Education Programs (OSEP) in the Office of Special Education and Rehabilitative Services (OSERS).

STATES REQUIRED ABOUT 2 PERCENT OF DISTRICTS NATIONWIDE TO PROVIDE EARLY INTERVENING SERVICES IN SCHOOL YEAR 2010-11

Among the almost 15,000 school districts nationwide that received IDEA funding in school year 2010-11, states required 356 (2.4 percent) districts to use these funds for early intervening services due to significant disproportionality. This represents a 12 percent decrease from the previous school year when 405 school districts were required to provide these services. Over half of the districts required to provide services in both school years were concentrated in five states—Louisiana, Michigan, Mississippi, New York, and Rhode Island—with 73 districts located in Louisiana alone in school year 2010-11. Twenty-one states did not require any of their districts to provide services (see fig. 2).

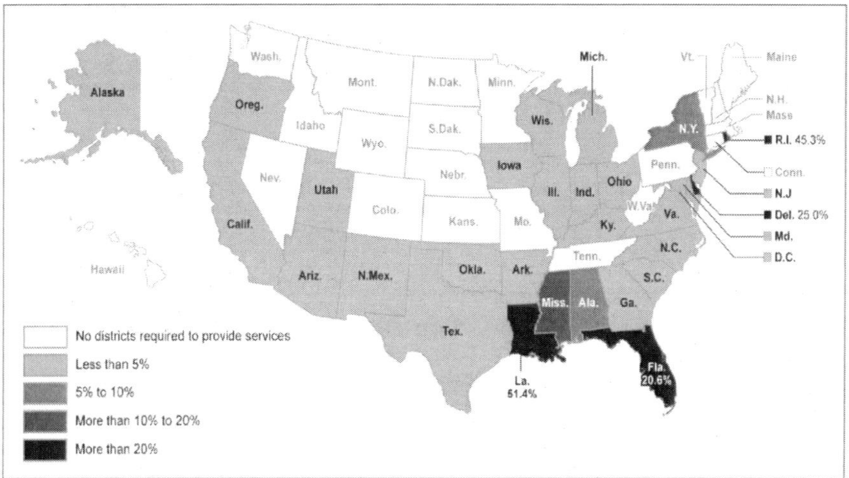

Source: GAO analysis of Education's IDEA Table 8 data file as of August 13, 2012; National Atlas of the United States (base map).

Figure 2. Percentage of Districts Required to Provide Early Intervening Services by State (School Year 2010-11).

An additional 9 percent of districts nationwide that were not identified as having significant disproportionality voluntarily provided these services in school year 2010-11, but that number similarly decreased from 1,508 (about 10 percent) in school year 2009-10 to 1,265 (about 9 percent) in 2010-11 (see fig. 3). In total, about 1.26 million students received early intervening services during the 2010-11 school year. See appendix II for state-by-state data on the number of children served and number and percentage of districts providing services in the 2009-10 and 2010-11 school years.

The characteristics of students in the districts that were required to and voluntarily provided early intervening services did not differ substantially, except that the districts required to provide services had a higher percentage of African American students and a lower percentage of Hispanic students (see fig. 4).

However, given the small number of districts required to provide services, it may be difficult to discern meaningful differences between these two groups of districts, which also differed little from the majority of districts providing no services, as shown below.

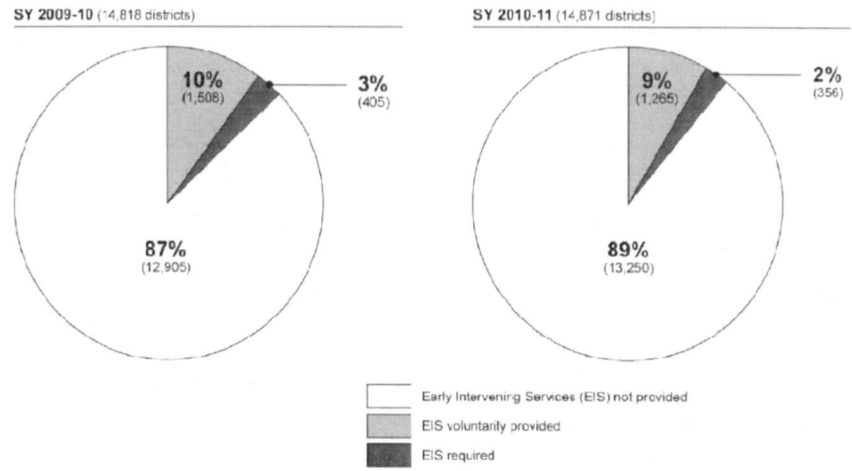

Source: Education's IDEA Table 8 data file as of January 24, 2012 for ST2009-2010 and August 13, 2012 to SY2010-2011.

Notes: Percentages may not add to 100 percent due to rounding. SY = school year.

Figure 3. Number and Percentage of Districts Providing Early Intervening Services (School Years 2009-10 and 2010-11).

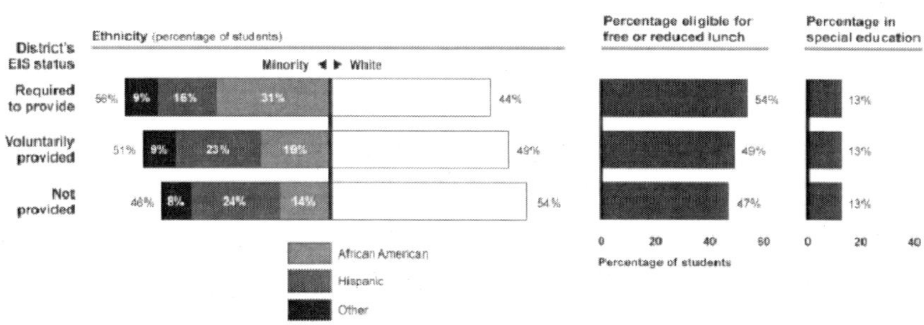

Source: GAO analysis of Education's IDEA Table 8 data file as of August 13, 2012 and Common Care of Data as of August 20, 2012.

Figure 4. Selected Characteristics of Districts by Provision of Early Intervening Services (School Year 2010-11).

During the 2 school years we reviewed, districts also reduced funding reserved for early intervening services, as shown in table 2. Funding decreased 47 percent between school years 2009-10 and 2010-11 among districts required to provide services and more steeply—56 percent—among districts voluntarily providing services.[10]

Table 2. Amount of IDEA, Part B Funding Reserved for Early Intervening Services (School Years 2009-10 and 2010-11)

Type of district	Number of districts SY 2009-10	Amount of IDEA funding reserved SY 2009-10	Percentage of total IDEA funding SY 2009-10	Number of districts SY 2010-11	Amount of IDEA funding reserved SY 2010-11	Percentage of total IDEA funding SY 2010-11	Percentage change in amount reserved from SY 2009-10 to SY 2010-11
Districts required to provide services	405	$306,949,685	1.44	356	$163,851,707	1.60	-47
Districts voluntarily providing services	1,508	$251,840,189	1.18	1,265	$110,175,488	1.07	-56
Total	1,913	$558,789,874	2.62	1,621	$274,027,195	2.67	-51

Source: GAO analysis of Education's IDEA Table 8 data file as of January 24, 2012 for SY 2009-10 and August 13, 2012 for SY 2010-11.

Note: SY = School Year.

Table 3. Key Components of Definitions of Significant Disproportionality in Identification for 16 Selected States

State	Value to be exceeded when comparing groups	Years value must be exceeded	SY 09-10	SY 10-11	Districts in state SY 10-11
			Districts required to provide early intervening services		
Alaska	3.5 or more	3 consecutive years	0	1	54
California	4.0 or more a	Current year and 2 out of 3 previous years	17	15	980
Connecticut	4.0 or more	2 consecutive years	3	0	169
Delaware	1.4 (decreasing each year based on stakeholder input)	2 consecutive years	15	9	36
Florida	3.50 or more	1year	13	15	72
Iowa	2.0 or more	3 consecutive years	7	7	376
Louisiana	2.0 or more	1 year	86	73	111
Maryland	2.0 or more in 4 of 6 disability categories	1 year	8	1	25
Mississippi	4.0 or more	1 year	35	28	151
Nebraska	3.0 or more	2 consecutive years	0	0	253
Pennsylvania	Greater than 4.0	3 consecutive years	0	0	615
Rhode Island	Risk level for group being examined 1% or higher than the national risk for all students and a risk ratio at least 2.5 times the combined risk for all students in the nation	2 consecutive years	26	24	51
South Carolina	4.0 or more	1 year	3	4	85
Texas	Calculated value must exceed critical value set by state. Critical value set at 99th percentile	2 consecutive years	5	12	1259
West Virginia	3.0 or more	2 consecutive years	0	0	57
Wisconsin	4.0 or more and risk 1.0% or greater than state level risk for white students	3 consecutive years	2	5	446

Source: GAO analysis of 16 selected state definitions of significant disproportionality. For the number of districts in state, Education's IDEA Table 8 data file as of January 24, 2012 for SY 2009-10 and August 13, 2012 for SY 2010-11. In addition to a risk ratio, California uses an additional calculation called an E-formula, which assesses whether the proportion of the group in special education being examined exceeds the proportion of that same group in general education by 3 standard errors.

Note: SY = School Year.

Some officials we interviewed said that the additional funding districts received under the Recovery Act,[11] which gave states an additional $11.7 billion for IDEA, enabled them to fund early intervening services, but without these funds school districts officials said they struggled to provide these services without major cuts to other educational services. For example, in California's Capistrano Unified School District, officials reported that they eliminated approximately 50 positions to pay for these services, and the student-teacher ratio increased from 20:1 to 32:1. In Baltimore County School District, officials reported that they will be required to use about $3.3 million of IDEA, Part B funds for these services in school year 2012-13, and because they must also provide special education services, general education teachers and general education services will likely be affected.

State-Developed Criteria Largely Drives Decisions about Whether Districts Are Required to Provide Early Intervening Services

Selected states' definitions for determining which districts have significant disproportionality—and are required to provide early intervening services—varied widely and may prevent states from identifying the magnitude of racial and ethnic overrepresentation in special education, according to our analysis. To determine whether any of their districts have significant disproportionality, states have used the flexibility Education provided them to develop their own definitions. These definitions include method(s) of calculation and associated criteria that set the conditions under which a determination of significant disproportionality is made. Specifically, after states calculate how many students of each race and ethnicity receive special education services, states compare these results to criteria established in their definition, which include (1) the value that must be exceeded, and (2) the number of years that value or condition must persist for a determination of significant disproportionality. States can also establish a minimum number of students needed in a group for calculation, and all of these factors can influence a determination of significant disproportionality.[12] In general, the higher the value that must be exceeded, the more years the value or condition must persist, and the greater the minimum number of students required for calculation, the less likely a state will identify districts as having significant disproportionality. (See table 3).

The following examples illustrate how state definitions can influence the extent to which districts are found to have significant disproportionality.

Pennsylvania, a state with almost 1.8 million students and 16 percent of its students receiving special education services, did not require any of its over 600 districts to provide services in either of the years we examined.[13] In this state, racial and ethnic groups in a district must be identified for special education at a rate more than four times higher than other groups for 3 consecutive years to be identified as having significant disproportionality. Pennsylvania also requires districts to have at least 40 students in each racial and ethnic group to conduct a calculation— allowing small districts and districts with small numbers of certain racial and ethnic groups to be exempt from providing services since the districts are excluded from the calculation of significant disproportionality. Similarly, in Nebraska, which has about 300,000 school-age children, of which 15 percent receive special education services, none of the state's 253 districts were identified as having significant disproportionality in school years 2009-10 or 2010-11. In this state, racial and ethnic groups in any of its districts must be identified in a specific disability category at a rate three times higher than all students for 2 successive years to trigger the requirement for services, and districts must have at least 30 students in a racial or ethnic group to be included in their calculations. Alaska, a state with over 132,000 school-age children, of which 14 percent receive special education, required none of its 54 districts to provide services in school year 2009-10 and one district in 2010-11. In Alaska, racial and ethnic groups in the district must be identified for special education at a rate three-and-a-half times higher than their non-minority peers for 3 consecutive years.

In contrast, states such as Louisiana, Maryland, and Rhode Island identified relatively more districts that were required to provide early intervening services. For example, Louisiana, a state with 700,000 school-age children, required 86 of its 111 districts to provide services in school year 2009-10, and 73 in school year 2010-11. In that state, if racial and ethnic groups are found to be identified for special education at twice the rate of other students in a district, in a single year, it must provide services. Maryland, a state with 850,000 school-age children, required 8 of its 25 districts to provide services in school year 2009-10, although that number dropped to one in 2010-11. In Maryland, districts must provide services when racial and ethnic groups are represented two or more times the rate of students who are in four out of six disability categories in any year. Finally, Rhode Island, a state with 143,000 students, of which 18 percent are in special education, required 26 of its 51 districts to provide services in school year 2009-10 and 24 in school year 2010-11. In that state, services are required in districts where racial and ethnic groups are two and half times more than the combined risk of all students in the nation for 2 consecutive years to be in special education. (See fig. 5.)

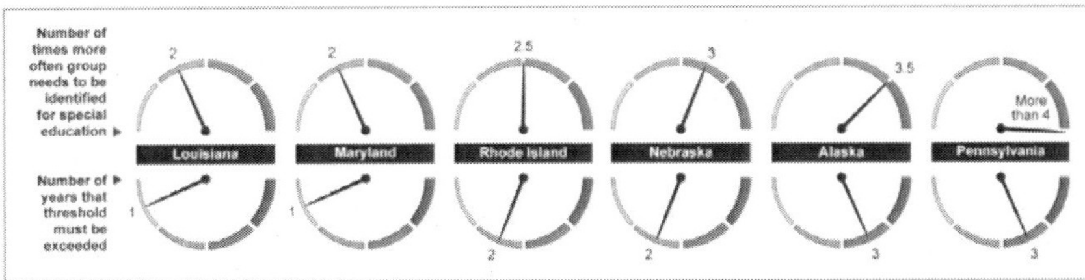

Source: GAO analysis of selected states' definitions of significant disproportionality.

Figure 5. Differences in State Definitions of Significant Disproportionality, Selected Elements.

In addition to the key components of a state's definition, the method of calculation can affect whether a district is identified as having significant disproportionality and required to provide early intervening services. States have discretion to select the methods for calculating significant disproportionality. For example, one commonly used set of methods examines "risk" of being in special education. This includes calculation of risk, risk ratios, alternate risk ratios, and weighted risk ratios. Some of these methods compare students within a district while others compare students in the district with students in the state or the nation. These comparisons can be of students in the same racial group within the district or compare one racial group from the district to that racial group at the state or national level. Also, with one method, the calculated value might be above the value and the district would be identified as having significant disproportionality, whereas with another method, it might not. To illustrate the effect a state's choice of methodology can have on a finding of significant disproportionality, we applied Louisiana's methodology, a risk ratio, to state data from Nebraska, which identified no districts. We found that in school year 2010-11, African American students in Nebraska were identified with emotional disabilities at a rate 2.9 times higher than all other students in the state.[14] However, because Nebraska's criteria for significant disproportionality requires districts to have over-identified students of a racial or ethnic group 3 times more often than other groups combined, no districts were required to provide services for the years we reviewed.[15] The reverse was also true when we applied Nebraska's criterion to Louisiana's state data. African American students in Louisiana were identified at a rate 2.2 times more often for intellectual disabilities than all other students in the state in school year 2010-11. While this rate is considered significantly disproportionate using Louisiana's criteria it would not be considered significantly disproportionate using Nebraska's criteria. (See app. I for more information on our methodology and app. III for more detailed information on the definitions used in the 16 states we reviewed.)

We explored the reasons some states adopted their definitions of significant disproportionality. In some states, such as Maryland and Florida, officials reported they have chosen to reduce burden or confusion by defining significant disproportionality in the same way they define other IDEA annual reporting requirements on disproportionality. For example, in Maryland the definitions for significant disproportionality and disproportionate representation of racial and ethnic groups in special education are the same.[16] Other states opted for a tiered approach, setting certain criteria of the definition of significant disproportionality higher than other IDEA reporting requirements on disproportionality. For example, in Alaska, districts are considered as having significant disproportionality when racial and ethnic groups are identified for special education at a rate three-and-a-half times higher than their non-minority peers, whereas for disproportionate representation, the requirement is that they be three times more likely. Finally, California conducted extensive research to determine the strengths and weaknesses of various definitions and ran different scenarios in all of their districts to determine outcomes from each definition. Based on this analysis, the state developed a new methodology so complex an Education official reported the monitoring team needed a substantial amount of time for its review.

DISTRICTS PROVIDED A RANGE OF SERVICES TO ASSIST STRUGGLING STUDENTS

The types of early intervening services students received varied, according to a national study by Education,[17] with most districts providing literacy instruction; response to intervention (RTI), an approach that provides different levels of assistance to students based on their needs; [18] and behavioral interventions (see table 4.)

Table 4. Percentage of Districts Providing Early Intervening Services Using IDEA, Part B Funds, by the Type of Activity Funded (School Year 2008–2009)

Type of activity supported by IDEA, Part B program funds	Districts required to provide early intervening services (percentage)	Districts voluntarilyproviding earlyintervening services(percentage)
Literacy instruction	81.79	84.33
Response to Intervention (RTI)	81.65	67.07
Behavioral interventions	63.36	60.11
Math instruction	63.22	48.63
Adaptive and instructional software	55.02	41.43
Educational evaluations	43.00	46.30
Behavioral evaluations	47.47	36.51
Other instruction	17.79	21.23
Other	14.06	10.76

Source: Education's 2011 IDEA National Assessment Implementation Study.

The districts we visited also reported providing these services using IDEA funds. Most of the districts we visited reported providing supplemental instruction in reading and math. For instance, the Austin Independent School District in Texas implemented a program for middle school students who were up to two grade levels behind and found that a higher number of participating students passed the state's standardized math test. Officials from Baltimore County School District in Maryland reported that fifth graders who participated in a before-school program increased their math test scores. In Duval County School District, Florida, officials reported that the district provided elementary school students who faced significant academic challenges—including students who had been held back—with individualized math and reading instruction that resulted in improved performance on state assessments.

Most districts we visited also provided services to address students' behavioral and emotional issues, which can affect learning. For example, in Prince George's County School District, Maryland, officials reported that behavior specialists were placed in the middle and high schools with the highest number of suspensions to help students develop skills such as coping and anger management. The specialists also worked with teachers to help them identify alternative strategies to address student misconduct. In the Jefferson County School District in Florida, officials reported that school staff worked with middle school and high school students to develop plans and interventions to address attendance, tardiness, and behavior problems.

Officials from two districts we visited said that providing students more assistance with literacy can also help address their behavior problems. As one official noted, students are less likely to act out if they feel more successful academically.

Teachers' perceptions about students can also play a role in special education placement, and most of the districts we visited reported using IDEA funds for their professional development and for other school staff. For example, in Baltimore County School District, Maryland, officials reported that principals will take training in cultural awareness to help them better discern the underlying reasons for the behavior a child may be exhibiting and understand that the behavior may not necessarily indicate the need for placement in special education. District officials from all eight districts we visited cited improved decision-making in that providing the services allowed them to more readily assess whether students were responding to the services or needed more intensive services, such as those provided through special education. Officials from all eight districts we visited also reported that referrals for special education evaluations still occurred, but where there was ambiguity, early intervening services allowed them to see if the child benefited from the services. For example, officials from Liberty School District in Texas said that although some students showed no improvement with early intervening services, the information staff collected while providing the services allowed them to more accurately identify children who needed special education services. Officials from the Jefferson County School District in Florida told us these services allowed them to collect better data on children's progress and now they better distinguish students who need more help in the general classroom from those who need special education services.

Inconsistent Definitions and Limited Oversight May Hinder Identification of Overrepresentation of Racial and Ethnic Groups in Special Education

Federal Oversight

Education has responsibility for monitoring overrepresentation of racial and ethnic groups in special education. However, Education's ability to oversee states' identification of districts with significant disproportionality is hampered by the flexibility states have to individually define significant disproportionality. Rather than developing a standard definition of significant disproportionality that all states could use, Education told states they have the discretion to define the term, citing the need to give states flexibility to account for factors such as population size and composition.[19] However, during the course of our study, Education officials acknowledged that some states' definitions may be preventing them from identifying disproportionality. According to Education officials, the requirement for districts identified with significant disproportionality to reserve 15 percent of their IDEA, Part B funds for early intervening services could be a financial burden, a sentiment echoed by officials in several states and districts we visited, who saw the requirement as a struggle for districts to afford.

In addition, while Education requires states to change their definition of significant disproportionality when it appears to treat one racial or ethnic group differently, it has not similarly required states to change their definitions when they make it unlikely that disproportionality will be identified. As part of its on-site monitoring of IDEA, Education reviews each state's definition approximately every 5 years, but does not currently collect these definitions even though states can change their definitions annually. In reviewing states' definitions, Education officials told us they assess whether the definitions appear to treat one racial or ethnic group differently and the department may solicit input from its Office for Civil Rights when making such determinations.[20] We found that in 2010 Education required California to revise its definition because of such concerns. However, Education officials also said the department generally has not required states to change their definition even when an assessment suggests that a state's definition may prevent it from identifying overrepresentation of racial and ethnic groups in special education. For example, when Education concluded that Alaska's definition made it unlikely that any districts would be identified, it did not require the state to change its definition but suggested only that Alaska reexamine its definition. During our review, Education officials acknowledged that state definitions of significant disproportionality merit additional attention, and in response to issues we have raised, said over the next year they will begin collecting states' definitions and examine race and ethnicity data to establish whether states' current definitions appropriately gauge disproportionality. Education officials also said they are considering other options to gather information to address concerns that states' definitions might be masking overrepresentation of racial and ethnic groups, including auditing states that have not identified any districts and providing guidance to states.

However, Education has not articulated how it will address the differing definitions states currently have for defining significant disproportionality that prevent the Department from having a consistent picture of the extent of the problem.

In addition to reviewing states' definitions during on-site monitoring visits, Education recently began collecting data on districts providing early intervening services. In 2011, Education began collecting such data for the 2009-10 school year regarding early intervening services. These data include the number of districts required to provide services, the amount of IDEA funds reserved, the number of students receiving services, and the number of students who subsequently received special education. However, at the time of our review, Education officials had not used the data to specifically inform their review of definitions of states with no identified districts. Instead, Education officials reported that they review the data to check for its accuracy and signs of possible noncompliance with the law. For instance, Education officials reported that they flag districts that did not reserve funds for early intervening services, but reported students receiving these services. Education officials said that they contact the state and district to ensure the data are accurate and, if noncompliance is identified, to ensure corrective action is taken.

Education also monitors overrepresentation of racial and ethnic groups in special education through three performance indicators, based on monitoring priorities prescribed in IDEA. The three indicators Education uses are: (1) "disproportionate representation" of racial and ethnic groups in special education due to inappropriate identification, (2) "disproportionate representation" of racial and ethnic groups in special education in specific disability categories due to inappropriate identification, and (3) "significant discrepancies" in suspensions and expulsions (see appendix IV). While these indicators use different terminology, they overlap with the requirement for states to identify significant disproportionality. For instance, states must identify whether racial and ethnic groups are disproportionately identified for special education and by category of impairment when calculating both significant disproportionality and disproportionate representation. As with the flexibility states have in developing their definitions of significant disproportionality, states have discretion in how they define disproportionate representation and significant discrepancy. Therefore, one state may have different definitions across these measures of overrepresentation and therefore different findings of overrepresentation (see fig.6), while another state may have the same definitions. In addition to the data states submit to Education on early intervening services, states must also annually report on these indicators. While we were unable to fully explore this issue in our current study, we recently reported that state and school districts officials we interviewed found Education's IDEA indicators to be complicated, resource-intensive, and duplicative.[21] Education has sought input from state special education directors on this issue. The majority of state directors Education surveyed supported the idea of having one requirement to identify overrepresentation of racial and ethnic groups among districts instead of requirements for identifying both significant disproportionality and disproportionate representation.

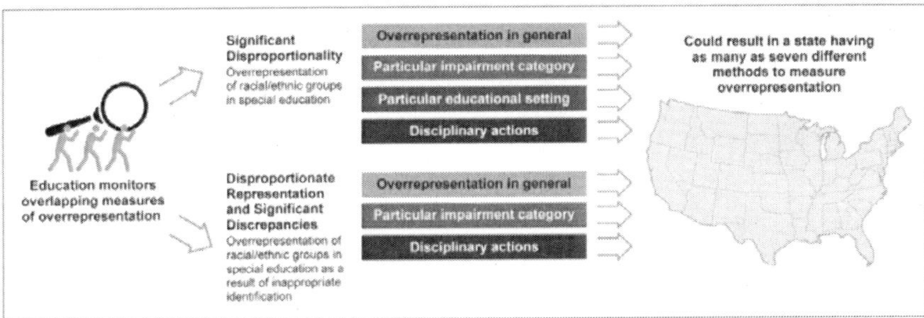

Source: GAO analysis of Education's guidance for early intervening services and IDEA indicators.

Figure 6. Overlap between IDEA Performance Indicators and Significant Disproportionality.

State Oversight

States are responsible for identifying the districts required to provide services and then ensuring that these districts spend the required 15 percent of IDEA funds for these services (see fig. 7 on state oversight role). To carry out its responsibilities, officials in the states we visited reported various monitoring activities to oversee districts' fiscal compliance and service implementation. For example, to monitor fiscal compliance in California, officials reported using accounting codes to track districts' use of IDEA funds for early intervening services. Maryland officials said they conduct periodic on-site monitoring of districts. In Texas, state officials said districts that have significant disproportionality are required to use their data to determine the root causes of overrepresentation and that the state's data system facilitates this analysis by allowing districts to examine their data in a variety of ways.

States we visited also had different approaches for overseeing the types of services provided. Two of the states we visited reported requiring those districts to submit to the state a plan for how they will implement early intervening services, including the services they will provide. In Florida, officials said that districts are required to use funds for direct student support services, rather than for curriculum materials or administrative supports, and that the state reviews districts' plans and provides additional guidance to ensure districts follow this state requirement.

Maryland officials, in contrast, said that they do not dictate how districts deliver services to their students.

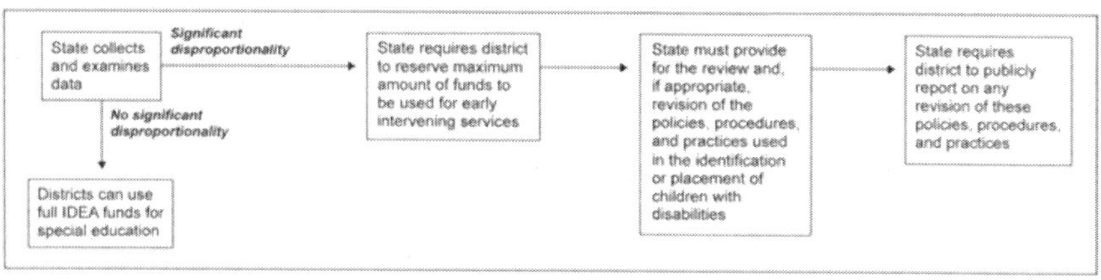

Source: GAO analysis of IDEA.

Figure 7. State Role in Overseeing Early Intervening Services.

CONCLUSION

To address the persistent problem of the overrepresentation of racial and ethnic groups in special education, Congress required states and school districts to take measures to help improve outcomes for struggling students. However, the discretion that states have in defining significant disproportionality has resulted in a wide range of definitions that provides no assurance that the problem is being appropriately identified across the nation. More significantly, without these services, struggling students may not receive the services they need to help them improve academically and thus may ultimately need special education services. Education has allowed states the flexibility to define significant disproportionality to account for differences in state population size and composition. However, a standard approach to defining significant disproportionality with built-in flexibilities to account for differences among states, would provide better assurance that states are gauging the true magnitude of the problem of overrepresentation of racial and ethnic groups in special education.

RECOMMENDATION FOR EXECUTIVE ACTION

To better understand the extent of racial and ethnic overrepresentation in special education and promote consistency in how states determine the districts required to provide early intervening services, we recommend the Secretary of Education develop a standard approach for defining significant disproportionality to bc used by all states. This approach should allow flexibility to account for state differences and specify when exceptions can be made.

AGENCY COMMENTS AND OUR EVALUATION

We provided a draft of this report to the Department of Education for review and comment. In its comments, Education stated that the effect of state definitions of significant disproportionality on decisions concerning children from various racial and ethnic groups merit additional attention. However, in response to our recommendation that the department require a standard approach to define significant disproportionality to be used by all states, Education proposed an alternative course of action that would focus on more collection of information about state definitions and to make that information available to the public as a matter of transparency. Specifically, Education stated that for the upcoming reporting year, the department will collect states' definitions of significant disproportionality and information by disability categories in which a district was identified with significant disproportionality. Education stated that such information will provide greater transparency and assist in holding states accountable for meeting the requirements regarding significant disproportionality and early intervening services by highlighting states where further examination may be warranted. Further, the department said that it may provide additional guidance on the issue that might include developing a standard approach for defining significant disproportionality. While the department's data collection efforts will allow it to have, for the first time, complete information about the full range of definitions states are using, our report provides several examples of the range of different ways states have defined significant disproportionality. We believe that Education's proposed efforts do little to address the overriding concern raised in our study about the lack of consistency across states in how they define significant disproportionality. Further, because some state definitions can be very complex and states can change definitions annually, we are concerned that Education's collection and review of definitions may be burdensome for it to execute. Consequently, we have not revised our recommendation.

Education also provided technical comments which we incorporated into the report where appropriate.

George A. Scott
Director,
Education, Workforce, and Income Security Issues

Appendix I: Scope and Methodology

This appendix discusses our methodology for this study, which was framed around three objectives: (1) What are the numbers and characteristics of districts that provide early intervening services and how do states determine which districts are required to provide services? (2) What are the types of services provided? (3) How do the Department of Education (Education) and states oversee early intervening services?

Providing Information on the Numbers and Characteristics of Districts and How States Identify Districts for Early Intervening Services

To determine the number and characteristics of districts providing early intervening services, we analyzed Education's IDEA data, commonly referred to as Table 8 data, for 2009-10 and 2010-11, the most recent years at the time of our review, and IDEA, Part B data on child counts (618 data). We analyzed data reported by the states to Education on the number of districts providing services and the amount of IDEA, Part B funding districts reserved for these services. To create a composite description of districts, we linked information from Table 8 on the characteristics of the districts that were required to and voluntarily provided services, as well as districts that did not provide early intervening services, to data from Education's Common Core of Data for school year 2010-11, which includes the characteristics of all students enrolled in the school districts, including their racial/ethnic composition, percentage receiving special education, and percentage eligible for free or reduced price lunch. To assess the reliability of data from these data sets, we interviewed relevant Education officials, reviewed documentation of data collection procedures, and conducted internal reliability checks. We determined that the data were sufficiently reliable for our purposes.

To determine how states determine which districts are required to provide services, we collected and reviewed 16 states' methodologies for determining significant disproportionality with respect to the percentages of racial and ethnic groups in special education, which triggers the requirement that districts provide services.

To ensure that our review of 16 states included states with districts that did and did not have districts identified as having significant disproportionality, we chose the six states with the highest percentage of districts required to provide services in school year 2009-10 (Delaware, Florida, Louisiana, Maryland, Mississippi and Rhode Island), and eight additional states (Alaska, Connecticut, Iowa, Nebraska, Pennsylvania, South Carolina, West Virginia, and Wisconsin) that we selected through a stratified, random sample, based on the number of districts required to provide early intervening services.[1]

Texas and California were selected because they were included in our site visit selection and due to their relatively low percentage of districts required to provide services in School Year 2009-10. The selected states were Alaska, California, Connecticut, Delaware, Florida, Iowa, Louisiana, Maryland, Mississippi, Nebraska, Pennsylvania, Rhode Island, South Carolina, Texas, West Virginia, and Wisconsin. We requested each state's definition and analyzed them with respect to their method(s) of calculation, the minimum number of students in a group required for performing the calculation (N size), the number of years of data used, and the threshold value for identification of significant disproportionality. We followed up with knowledgeable officials in the 16 states to ensure our analysis was accurate and up to date.

Further, in order to illustrate how a state's choice of definition can affect a finding of significant disproportionality, we provide two scenarios in the report using state data from Nebraska and Louisiana. To do this, we applied a standard metric, a risk ratio, to Louisiana and Nebraska's state data. To reduce the risk of inappropriately identifying a particular racial or ethnic group for receiving special education services, different methodologies for assessing risk can be used in calculating disproportionality.

As part of our review, we chose to assess the risk of racial and ethnic student groups being placed in special education using a general risk ratio analysis applied to data from Education's Common Core of Data. We conducted these analyses on school year 2010-11 state level data to determine the rate of racial and ethnic groups' identification for special education, and for each disability category. According to the Department of Education, this risk ratio method of calculation is used to answer the question: "What is a specific racial/ethnic group's risk of receiving special education and related services for a particular disability compared to the risk for all other children with that disability?"

Using this method, we calculated a risk ratio value, which we then compared to a "cut point" number which is determined by the state. The cut point number indicates how much more likely students of a specific race or ethnicity have to be overrepresented in special education in order for districts in a state to be considered as having significant disproportionality. The calculated risk ratio value has to be greater than the cut point value for a specific racial/ethnic group's risk to be considered significantly disproportionate. States can vary in the cut point number they choose to use and, in our analyses, we examined the risk ratio values we calculated in relation to the cut points used by Nebraska and Louisiana.

Describing the Types of Services Provided

To identify the types of early intervening services districts provided, we reviewed Education's IDEA National Assessment Implementation Study, which included national data on the types of early intervening services districts provided during the 2008-09 school year.[2] To gain further insight into how these services were delivered at the school and district level, we conducted site visits in four of our 16 selected states—California, Florida, Maryland, and Texas. In each state, we interviewed officials from the state department of education and two school districts we visited. In three states, we also visited elementary schools (see table 5.) We selected these states based on geography, the percentage of districts required to implement the program, and the percentage of districts that implemented the program voluntarily. Within these states, we selected the districts based on location, whether they were required to or voluntarily provided services, the amount they received in IDEA, Part B funding, poverty levels, percentage of students receiving special education services, and size. The information provided from these four site visits is not generalizeable across all states and school districts.

Table 5. Early Intervening Services Provided in the Districts We Visited

District	Student enrollment (School Year 2010-11)	Required or Voluntarily Providing Services	Amount reserved and percent of IDEA, Part B allocation	Number of children served	Schools Visited
Capistrano Unified School District, CA	53,192	Required in SY 2009-10 and SY 2010-11	For SY 2009-10: $ 2,830,881 (15%) For SY 2010-11: $1,290,287 (15%)	Not reported	Palisades Elementary
Chico Unified School District, CA	13,060	Voluntarily in SY 2009-10 Not required or provided voluntarily in SY 2010-11	$85,000 (2%)	154	Chapman and Shasta ElementarySchools
Duval County, FL	123,997	Voluntarily in SY 2009-10 Not required or provided voluntarily in SY 2010-11	$2,117,879 (3%)	1,304	Jacksonville Heights Elementary
Jefferson County, FL	1,104	Required in SY 2009-10 and SY 2010-11	For SY 2009-10: $124,625 (15%) For SY 2010-11: $72,814 (15%)	For 2009-10: 84 For 2010-11: 142	Jefferson County ESE Combination School
Baltimore County Public Schools, MD	104,160	Required in SY 2009-10 Not required or provided voluntarily in SY 2010-11	$7,402,321 (15%)	4,105	No schools visited
Prince George's County Public Schools, MD	126,671	Not required or provided voluntarily in SY 2009-10 Required in SY 2010-11	$3,859,783 (15%)	1,491	No schools visited
Austin Independent School District, TX	85,697	Voluntarily in SY 2009-10 Not required or provided voluntarily in SY 2010-11	$2,596,202 (8%)	604	Andrews Elementary School
Liberty Independent School District, TX	2,148	Required in SY 2009-10 Not required or provide voluntarily in SY 2010-11	$138,404 (15%)	103	San Jacinto Elementary School

Sources: Education's IDEA data and Common Core of Data.

Note: SY = School Year.

Identifying How Education and States Oversee Early Intervening Services

To determine how Education and states oversee the provision of early intervening services, we interviewed Education officials from the Office of Special Education Programs (OSEP) and Office for Civil Rights.

We interviewed staff from Education's contractor for its Data Accountability Center[3] that at the time of our review was responsible for providing technical assistance to states in developing the definitions of significant disproportionality, disproportionate representation, and significant discrepancy.

In addition, we interviewed members of Education's Disproportionality Priority Team, created under the umbrella of Education's Regional Resource Centers. This entity was established to help states address disproportionality in special education and is comprised of staff from OSEP, the Regional Resource Centers, and the Data Accountability Center.

We reviewed relevant federal laws and regulations and Education's monitoring policies and protocols. For the 16 states included in our review, we obtained and reviewed Education's findings from their most recent monitoring visits, all of which were conducted between 2008 and 2011.

We interviewed officials in the four states we visited about the states' monitoring activities, as well as their perspectives of Education's monitoring. We also interviewed a few experts in the field of racial disparities in special education, and staff at relevant organizations, including the Council for Exceptional Children and the National Association of State Directors of Special Education.

We conducted this performance audit from January 2012 to February 2013 in accordance with generally accepted government auditing standards.

Those standards require that we plan and perform the audit to obtain sufficient, appropriate evidence to provide a reasonable basis for our findings and conclusions based on our audit objectives.

We believe that the evidence obtained provides a reasonable basis for our findings and conclusions based on our audit objectives.

APPENDIX II: DATA ON THE NUMBER OF CHILDREN SERVED AND NUMBER AND PERCENTAGE OF DISTRICTS PROVIDING SERVICES BY STATE (SCHOOL YEARS 2009-10 AND 2010-11)

Table 6. Number of Children Receiving Early Intervening Services by State (School Years 2009-10 and 2010-11)

State	Total number of children receiving services (SY 2009-10)	Total number of children receiving services (SY 2010-11)
Alabama	1,055	2,880
Alaska	9,485	11,992
Arizona	45,221	32,779
Arkansas	5,654	5,051
California	10,892	32,633
Colorado	6,442	4,621

Table 6. Number of Children Receiving Early Intervening Services by State (School Years 2009-10 and 2010-11)

State	Total number of children receiving services (SY 2009-10)	Total number of children receiving services (SY 2010-11)
Connecticut	11,534	4,580
Delaware	19,676	22,573
District of Columbia	9	Not reported
Florida	67,292	75,776
Georgia	6,691	3,328
Hawaii	300	0
Idaho	3,060	406
Illinois	41,770	114,399
Indiana	14,956	21,298
Iowa	1,909	1,903
Kansas	73	53
Kentucky	902	2,658
Louisiana	82,048	79,953
Maine	0	0
Maryland	20,475	1,491

Table 6. (Continued)

State	Total number of children receiving services (SY 2009-10)	Total number of children receiving services (SY 2010-11)
Massachusetts	12,166	214
Michigan	15,851	16,792
Minnesota	2,215	2,993
Mississippi	45,637	36,660
Missouri	36,360	49,010
Montana	427	0
Nebraska	2,441	2,019
Nevada	65,577	72,239
New Hampshire	1,019	656
New Jersey	8,641	9,099
New Mexico	4,053	8,452
New York	101,221	142,642
North Carolina	43,128	47,780
North Dakota	3,780	1,813
Ohio	37,647	45,340
Oklahoma	27,565	29,641
Oregon	18,278	17,066
Pennsylvania	31,642	53,035
Rhode Island	7,385	8,674
South Carolina	50,576	30,858
South Dakota	759	1,083
Tennessee	32,379	6,312
Texas	229,404	200,065
Utah	12,240	7,242
Vermont	2,960	4,426
Virginia	11,294	10,738
Washington	10,345	13,417
West Virginia	240	138
Wisconsin	14,587	12,762
Wyoming	5,427	5,247
Total 50 states and D.C.	1,184,688	1,254,787

Source: GAO analysis of Education's IDEA Table 8 data file as of January 24, 2012 for SY2009-10 and August 13, 2012 for SY2010- 2011.

Note: SY = School Year.

Table 7. Number and Percentage of Districts Providing Early Intervening Services in the 2009-10 and 2010-11 School Years

State	Total number Of districts (2009-10)	Number Of districts required to provide services (2009-10)	Percentage of districts required to provide services (2009-10)	Number of districts voluntarily providing services (2009-10)	Percentage of districts voluntarily providing services (2009-10)	Total number of districts (2010-11)	Number Of districts required to provide services (2010-11)	Percentage of districts required to provide services (2010-11)	Number of Districts voluntarily providing services (2010-11)	Percentage of districts voluntarily providing services (2010-11)
Alabama	132	1	0.76%	3	2.27%	132	12	9.09%	4	3.03%
Alaska	54	0	0.00%	1	1.85%	54	1	1.85%	2	3.70%
Arizona	559	0	0.00%	62	11.09%	580	2	0.34%	37	6.38%
Arkansas	267	25	9.36%	53	19.85%	268	13	4.85%	35	13.06%
California	980	17	1.73%	7	0.71%	1,002	15	1.50%	5	0.50%
Colorado	61	0	0.00%	4	6.56%	62	0	0.00%	0	0.00%
Connecticut	169	3	1.78%	45	26.63%	169	0	0.00%	14	8.28%
Delaware	35	15	42.86%	0	0.00%	36	9	25.00%	0	0.00%
District of Columbia	46	5	10.87%	1	2.17%	43	1	2.33%	0	0.00%
Florida	72	13	18.06%	25	34.72%	73	15	20.55%	10	13.70%
Georgia	188	8	4.26%	9	4.79%	196	7	3.57%	7	3.57%
Hawaii	1	0	0.00%	1	100.00%	1	0	0.00%	0	0.00%
Idaho	127	0	0.00%	8	6.30%	131	0	0.00%	5	3.82%
Illinois	871	6	0.69%	96	11.02%	871	7	0.80%	203	23.31%
Indiana	355	7	1.97%	17	4.79%	354	7	1.98%	1	0.28%
Iowa	376	7	1.86%	6	1.60%	376	7	1.86%	8	2.13%
Kansas	78	0	0.00%	1	1.28%	76	0	0.00%	1	1.32%
Kentucky	176	4	2.27%	1	0.57%	176	7	3.98%	0	0.00%
Louisiana	111	86	77.48%	17	15.32%	142	73	51.41%	48	33.80%
Maine	315	0	0.00%	0	0.00%	290	0	0.00%	0	0.00%
Maryland	25	8	32.00%	1	4.00%	25	1	4.00%	1	4.00%

Table 7. (Continued)

State	Total number Of districts (2009-10)	Number Of districts required to provide services (2009-10)	Percentage of districts required to provide services (2009-10)	Number of districts voluntarily providing services (2009-10)	Percentage of districts voluntarily providing services (2009-10)	Total number of districts (2010-11)	Number Of districts required to provide services (2010-11)	Percentage of districts required to provide services (2010-11)	Number of Districts voluntarily providing services (2010-11)	Percentage of districts voluntarily providing services (2010-11)
Massachusetts	392	0	0.00%	23	5.87%	393	0	0.00%	5	1.27%
Michigan	717	11	1.53%	24	3.35%	731	29	3.97%	17	2.33%
Minnesota	251	0	0.00%	88	35.06%	256	0	0.00%	105	41.02%
Mississippi	151	35	23.18%	26	17.22%	151	28	18.54%	72	47.68%
Missouri	537	0	0.00%	8	1.49%	542	0	0.00%	11	2.03%
Montana	428	0	0.00%	0	0.00%	428	0	0.00%	0	0.00%
Nebraska	253	0	0.00%	14	5.53%	253	0	0.00%	10	3.95%
Nevada	17	0	0.00%	2	11.76%	17	0	0.00%	1	5.88%
New Hampshire	175	0	0.00%	16	9.14%	176	0	0.00%	7	3.98%
New Jersey	643	19	2.95%	12	1.87%	649	15	2.31%	11	1.69%
New Mexico	108	0	0.00%	13	12.04%	127	6	4.72%	13	10.24%
New York	701	63	8.99%	74	10.56%	701	40	5.71%	44	6.28%
North Carolina	213	1	0.47%	38	17.84%	217	2	0.92%	27	12.44%
North Dakota	32	0	0.00%	14	43.75%	32	0	0.00%	12	37.50%
Ohio	1,009	0	0.00%	116	11.50%	934	2	0.21%	96	10.28%
Oklahoma	532	21	3.95%	11	2.07%	529	2	0.38%	21	3.97%
Oregon	201	3	1.49%	18	8.96%	201	3	1.49%	19	9.45%
Pennsylvania	615	0	0.00%	26	4.23%	632	0	0.00%	16	2.53%
Rhode Island	51	26	50.98%	5	9.80%	53	24	45.28%	7	13.21%
South Carolina	85	3	3.53%	50	58.82%	86	4	4.65%	34	39.53%
South Dakota	159	0	0.00%	14	8.81%	156	0	0.00%	14	8.97%
Tennessee	139	0	0.00%	20	14.39%	139	0	0.00%	15	10.79%

State	Total number Of districts (2009-10)	Number Of districts required to provide services (2009-10)	Percentage of districts required to provide services (2009-10)	Number of districts voluntarily providing services (2009-10)	Percentage of districts voluntarily providing services (2009-10)	Total number of districts (2010-11)	Number Of districts required to provide services (2010-11)	Percentage of districts required to provide services (2010-11)	Number of Districts voluntarily providing services (2010-11)	Percentage of districts voluntarily providing services (2010-11)
Texas	1,259	5	0.40%	369	29.31%	1,253	12	0.96%	172	13.73%
Utah	114	2	1.75%	18	15.79%	117	1	0.85%	20	17.09%
Vermont	59	0	0.00%	17	28.81%	60	0	0.00%	16	26.67%
Virginia	132	5	3.79%	12	9.09%	132	6	4.55%	12	9.09%
Washington	295	0	0.00%	25	8.47%	295	0	0.00%	16	5.42%
West Virginia	57	0	0.00%	2	3.51%	57	0	0.00%	0	0.00%
Wisconsin	446	2	0.45%	72	16.14%	448	5	1.12%	67	14.96%
Wyoming	49	4	8.16%	23	46.94%	49	0	0.00%	24	48.98%

Source: GAO analysis of Education's IDEA Table 8 data file as of January 24, 2012 for SY2009-10 and August 13, 2012 for SY2010-2011.

Table 8. Student Enrollment and Number and Percentage of Students in Special Education by State (School Year 2010-11)

State	Student enrollment	Number of students in Special Education[a]	Percentage of students in Special Education[a]
AK	132,104	18,048	14
AL	755,552	81,216	11
AR	482,114	64,883	13
AZ	1,071,751	125,806	12
CA	6,289,578	662,508	11
CO	843,316	84,710	10
CT	560,546	68,130	12
DC	71,284	11,947	17
DE	129,403	18,608	14

Table 8. (Continued)

State	Student enrollment	Number of students in Special Education[a]	Percentage of students in Special Education[a]
FL	2,643,347	366,824	14
GA	1,677,067	177,536	11
HI	179,601	19,716	11
IA	495,775	68,498	14
ID	275,859	27,365	10
IL	2,091,654	303,092	14
IN	1,047,232	165,802	16
KS	483,701	66,851	14
KY	673,128	102,370	15
LA	696,558	82,934	12
MA	955,563	167,323	18
MD	852,211	102,818	12
ME	189,077	29,502	16
MI	1,587,067	217,213	14
MN	838,037	122,850	15
MO	918,710	127,148	14
MS	490,526	63,786	13
MT	141,693	16,760	12
NC	1,490,605	184,704	12
ND	96,323	13,097	14
NE	298,500	44,299	15
NH	194,711	29,778	15
NJ	1,402,548	225,471	16

State	Student enrollment	Number of students in Special Education[a]	Percentage of students in Special Education[a]
NM	338,122	46,612	14
NV	437,149	48,078	11
NY	2,734,955	452,551	17
OH	1,754,191	259,448	15
OK	659,911	97,247	15
OR	570,720	80,283	14
PA	1,793,284	295,077	16%
RI	143,793	25,332	18%
SC	725,838	100,262	14%
SD	126,128	18,026	14%
TN	987,422	119,004	12%
TX	4,935,715	441,987	9%
UT	585,552	70,232	12%
VA	1,251,440	162,338	13%
VT	96,858	13,562	14%
WA	1,043,788	127,909	12%
WI	872,286	124,721	14%
WV	282,879	44,924	16%
WY	89,009	15,231	17%

Source: GAO analysis of Education's Common Core of Data as of August 20, 2012.

[a] Students with Individualized Education Programs.

Appendix III: Criteria and Methodologies for Calculating Significant Disproportionality in 16 Selected States

State	Category of overrepresentation	Method of calculation	Minimum number in group required for performing the calculation (N size)	Threshold value for determination	Years threshold must be exceeded for determination
Alaska	Identification[a]	Risk Ratio	10 students with IEPs in the racial/ethnic group of interest AND in the comparison group	3.5 or more	3 consecutiveyears
	Placement	Risk Ratio	10 students with IEPs in the racial/ethnic group of interest AND the comparison group	3.5 or more	3 consecutiveyears
	Discipline	Risk Ratio	at least 10 children with IEPs enrolled in the school district	3.5 or more	3 consecutiveyears
California	Identification[a]	Alternate Risk Ratio and E Formula	20 plus	Ratio of 4.0 or more and E formula value exceeds 3 standard errors	Current Year & 2 out of 3 consecutive years
	Placement	Alternate Risk Ratio and E Formula	20 plus	Ratio of 4.0 or more and E formula value exceeds 3 standard errors	Current Year & 2 out of 3 consecutive years
	Discipline	State Rate of Suspension Plus 2%	20 plus	State Rate of Suspension Plus 2%	Current Year & 2 out of 3 consecutive years
Connecticut	Identificationa	Relative Risk Index	no minimum	4.0 or more	2 consecutiveyears
	Placement	Relative Risk Index	no minimum	4.0 or more	2 consecutiveyears
	Discipline	Relative Risk Index	no minimum	4.0 or more	2 consecutiveyears
Delaware	Identificationa	Relative Risk Ratio (beginning in school year 2011-12)	10	SY 2011-12 – 1.4 (decreasing each year based on stakeholder input)	2 consecutiveyears

State	Category of overrepresentation	Method of calculation	Minimum number in group required for performing the calculation (N size)	Threshold value for determination	Years threshold must be exceeded for determination
	Placement	Relative Difference Method	10	Relative difference value must be greater than .30	2 consecutiveyears
	Discipline	Rate Ratio	10	SY 09- 10 – 1.32; SY 10-11 – 1.3 (decreasing each year based on stakeholder input)	2 consecutiveyears
Florida	Identificationa	Risk Ratio	30 in group being examined	3.50 or more	Annually
	Placement	Risk Ratio	30 in group being examined	3.50 or more	Annually
	Discipline	Risk Ratio	30 incidents of removal in group being examined	3.50 or more	Annually
Iowa	Identificationa	Weighted Risk Ratio	10	2.0 or more	3 consecutiveyears
	Placement	Weighted Risk Ratio	10	2.5 or more	3 consecutiveyears
	Discipline	Rate of Suspension	10 with 3 or more students in the group being examined suspended/expelled for more than 10 days in the school year	2% above state average	3 consecutiveyears
Louisiana	Identificationa	Risk Ratio	10	2.0 or more	Annually
	Placement	Risk Ratio	10	2.0 or more	Annually
	Discipline	Comparison of Percents	no minimum	Percent must be higher than state average multiplied by 1.5	Annually
Maryland	Identificationa	Weighted Risk Ratio	30	2.0 or more in 4 of 6 disability categories	Annually
	Placement	Weighted Risk Ratio	30	2.0 or more	Annually
	Discipline	Comparative Discrepancy Ratio	30	2.0 or more	Annually
Mississippi	Identificationa	Alternate Risk Ratio	40 in group being examined	4.0 or more	Annually

Appendix III: (Continued)

State	Category of overrepresentation	Method of calculation	Minimum number in group required for performing the calculation (N size)	Threshold value for determination	Years threshold must be exceeded for determination
	Placement	Comparison of Percents	25 in group being examined	Percent must be higher than 2.0 times the state rate for students with disabilities in that placement	Annually
	Discipline	Comparison of Percents	20 students with disabilities suspended or expelled for more than 10 days in the school year	Percent must be more than 5 percentage points higher than the rate for all students without disabilities in the same school district.	Annually
Nebraska	Identificationa	Weighted Risk Ratio	30	3.0 or more	2 consecutiveyears
	Placement	Weighted Risk Ratio	30	3.0 or more	2 consecutiveyears
	Discipline	Comparison of Percents	30 with 6 or more students in the group being examined suspended/expelled for more than 10 days in the school year	Percent must be higher than 3.0 times the state rate for students with disabilities and 5.0 times state rate for race/ethnic groups	Annually
Pennsylvania	Identificationa	Weighted Risk Ratio	40	Greater than 4.0	3 consecutiveyears
	Placement	Weighted Risk Ratio	40	Greater than 4.0	3 consecutiveyears
	Discipline	Weighted Risk Ratio	40	Greater than 4.0	3 consecutiveyears

State	Category of overrepresentation	Method of calculation	Minimum number in group required for performing the calculation (N size)	Threshold value for determination	Years threshold must be exceeded for determination
Rhode Island	Identificationa	Risk Ratio	10 in group being examined	Risk level for group being examined 1% or higher than the national risk for all students and a risk ratio at least 2.5 times the combined risk for all students in the nation	2 consecutiveyears
	Placement	Alternate Risk Ratio or Alternate Total Removals Per Child (TRPC) Ratio plus E Formula	10 in group being examined	Ratio of 2.5 or more and E formula value exceeds 3 standard errors	2 consecutiveyears
	Discipline	Risk Ratio	10 in group being examined	Ratio of 2.5 or more and E formula value exceeds 3 standard errors	Annually
South Carolina	Identificationa	Weighted Risk Ratio	25	4.0 or more	Annually
	Placement	Weighted Risk Ratio	25	4.0 or more	Annually
	Discipline	Risk Ratio	25	4.0 or more in 2 or more of the disciplinary categories examined	Annually

Appendix III: (Continued)

State	Category of overrepresentation	Method of calculation	Minimum number in group required for performing the calculation (N size)	Threshold value for determination	Years threshold must be exceeded for determination
Texas	Identification [a]	Risk	Only school districts with at least 30 students receiving special education services are included in the computation of critical values and determination of disproportionality. Districts smaller than 100 students overall and districts with more than 40 percent of students receiving special education services are excluded	Calculated value must exceed critical value set by state. Critical value set at 99th percentile	2 consecutive years
	Placement	Risk	Only school districts with at least 30 students receiving special education services are included in the computation of critical values and determination of disproportionality. Districts smaller than 100 students overall and districts with more than 40 percent of students receiving special education services are excluded	Calculated value must exceed critical value set by state. Critical value set at 95th percentile	2 consecutive years
	Discipline	Risk	Only school districts with at least 30 students receiving special education services are included in the computation of critical values and determination of disproportionality. Districts smaller than 100 students overall and districts with more than 40 percent of students receiving special education services are excluded	Calculated value must exceed critical value set by state. Critical value set at 95th percentile	2 consecutive years
West Virginia	Identification [a]	Risk Ratio	20	3.0 or more	2 consecutive years

State	Category of overrepresentation	Method of calculation	Minimum number in group required for performing the calculation (N size)	Threshold value for determination	Years threshold must be exceeded for determination
	Placement	Risk Ratio	20	3.0 or more	2 consecutive years
	Discipline	Risk Ratio	20	3.0 or more	2 consecutive years
Wisconsin	Identification [a]	Weighted Risk Ratio	10 in group being examined and minimum total enrollment in the school district of 100 students in any given racial group being examined	4.0 or more and risk 1.0% or greater then state level risk for white students	3 consecutive years
	Placement	Weighted Risk Ratio	10 in group being examined and minimum total enrollment in the school district of 40 students in any given racial group being examined	4.0 or more and risk 1.0% or greater then state level risk for white students	3 consecutive years
	Discipline	Weighted Risk Ratio	10 in group being examined and minimum total enrollment in the school district of 40 students in any given racial group being examined	4.0 or more and risk 1.0% or greater then state level risk for white studen	3 consecutive years

Source: GAO analysis of information from state officials on selected states definitions of significant disproportionality.

[a]This includes identification and Identification in a specific disability category.

Appendix IV: Overlap between IDEA Indicators and Significant Disproportionality

IDEA Indicators *States required to determine annually:*	Significant Disproportionality *States must determine annually whether "significant disproportionality" based on race or ethnicity is occurring inthe State and LEAs of the State with respect to:*
"Disproportionate Representation" in Identification(Indicator 9): Percent of districts with disproportionate representation of racial and ethnic groups in special education and related services that is the result of inappropriate identification.	the identificationof children as children with disabilities;
"Disproportionate Representation" in Category(Indicator 10): Percent of districts with disproportionate representation of racial and ethnic groups in specific disability categories that is the result of inappropriate identification.	the identification of children with a particular disability;
	the placement of children with disabilities in particular educational settings; and
"Significant Discrepancy" in Discipline(Indicator 4b): Percent of districts that have a significant discrepancy, by race or ethnicity, in the rates of suspensions and expulsions of greater than 10 days in a school year for children with IEPs; and policies, procedures or practices that contribute to the significant discrepancy.	the incidence, duration, and type of disciplinary actions, including suspensions and expulsions.

Source: GAO analysis of Education's guidance for early intervening services and IDEA indicators.

End Notes

[1] Districts are allowed to use no more than 15 percent of their IDEA, Part B funds on early intervening services.

[2] Early intervening services and coordinated early intervening services are terms used interchangeably by Education. We use "early intervening services" throughout this report.

[3] IDEA data on early intervening services are collected by local educational agencies or educational service agencies. Throughout this report, use of the term "school districts" is synonymous with local educational agencies and educational service agencies.

[4] Data presented at the 2012 IDEA Leadership Conference: *Looking at Race/Ethnicity Disproportionality in Special Education from the Student Outcomes Side of the Educational System: Why Analyzing Disproportionality Matters for Results Improvement Planning (*Data Accountability Center and Regional Resource Center Program, Washington, D.C. 2012).

[5] Pub. L. No. 108-446, § 101, 118 Stat. 2647, 2739 (2004)(codified at 20 U.S.C. §§ 1413(f)(1) and 1418(d)(2)(B).

[6] The term "significant disproportionality" was used in the 1997 reauthorization of IDEA. At that time, Congress required states to collect and examine data to determine if significant disproportionality based on race is occurring with respect to the identification, particular disability category, and placement of students in special education. It was not until the 2004 reauthorization that Congress required districts identified as having significant disproportionality to use IDEA, Part B funds for early intervening services.

[7] 20 U.S.C. § 1413(f)(4).

[8] IDEA was originally enacted as the Education for All Handicapped Children Act, Pub. L. No. 94-142, 89 Stat. 773 (codified as amended at 20 U.S.C. §§ 1400-1482) (1975).

[9] See GAO, *Recovery Act: One Year Later, States and Localities' Use of Funds and Opportunities to Strengthen Accountability,* GAO-10-437 (Washington, D.C.: March 3, 2010).

[10] Education's data do not include information about the actual amount spent on these services. States have up to 27 months to obligate these funds for the provision of early intervening services.

[11] The American Recovery and Reinvestment Act of 2009 (Recovery Act) provided $11.7 billion in additional funding for IDEA, Part B grants to states and districts. School districts were required to obligate all IDEA Recovery Act funds by September 30, 2011. Education encouraged districts to spend the majority of these funds during the 2008-09 and 2009-10 school years.

[12] See app. III for detailed information on components of selected states' definitions for significant disproportionality.

[13] Pennsylvania reported it had 615 districts in SY 2009-10 and 632 districts in SY 2010-11.

[14] Nebraska uses a weighted risk ratio, not a general risk ratio as we used in our analysis, and resulting calculations of districts as having significant disproportionality using a general risk ratio may differ from our results. Further, our Louisiana calculation is based on state-wide data and resulting calculations of districts as having significant disproportionality may differ from Louisiana's state calculations. See app. III for detailed descriptions of state definitions for significant disproportionality.

[15] These comparisons are for illustrative purposes only and should not be construed to suggest that one methodology is preferable.

[16] Disproportionate representation is one of the IDEA annual performance indicators used to measure overrepresentation of racial and ethnic groups in special education.

[17] M.C. Bradley et al., *IDEA National Assessment Implementation Study* (NCEE 2011- 4027) (Washington, D.C.: National Center for Education Evaluation and Regional Assistance, Institute of Education Sciences, U. S. Department of Education, 2011. In this study, researchers surveyed a nationally representative sample of 1,200 school districts.

[18] For this study, response to intervention (RTI) was defined as a multi-step approach to providing early and progressively intensive intervention and monitoring within the general education setting. In principle, RTI begins with research-based instruction and behavioral support provided to students in the general education classroom, followed by screening of all students to identify those who may need systematic progress monitoring, intervention, or

support. Students who are not responding to the general education curriculum and instruction are provided with increasingly intense interventions through a tiered system, and they are frequently monitored to assess their progress and inform the choice of future interventions, including possibly special education for students determined to have a disability.

[19] Education discussed states' discretion in a 2007 memo to state special education directors and in the comment section of final agency regulations published in 2006. 71 Fed. Reg. 46,540, 46,738 (Aug. 14, 2006).

[20] Education's Office for Civil Rights enforces a number of civil rights laws including Title VI of the Civil Rights Act of 1964, which prohibits discrimination on the basis of race, color, or national origin under federally funded programs or activities.

[21] See GAO- K-12 *Education: Selected States and School Districts Cited Numerous Federal Requirements As Burdensome, While Recognizing Some Benefits,* GAO-12-672 (Washington, D.C.: June 27, 2012).

End Notes for Appendix I

[1] We randomly selected four states from those that identified some districts as significantly disproportionate (Iowa, Connecticut, South Carolina, and Wisconsin); and four states from those that did not identify any districts as significantly disproportionate (Alaska, Nebraska, Pennsylvania, and West Virginia.)

[2] M.C. Bradley et al., *IDEA National Assessment Implementation Study* (NCEE 2011- 4027) (Washington, D.C.: National Center for Education Evaluation and Regional Assistance, Institute of Education Sciences, U. S. Department of Education, 2011). In this study, researchers surveyed a nationally representative sample of 1,200 school districts.

[3] The Data Accountability Center was funded by Education to review IDEA data collection efforts and provide technical assistance to improve state capacity to meet data requirements.

In: Individuals with Disabilities Education Act ISBN: 978-1-62808-180-0
Editor: Harold Sanders

Chapter 2

THE INDIVIDUALS WITH DISABILITIES EDUCATION ACT (IDEA), PART B: KEY STATUTORY AND REGULATORY PROVISIONS*

Ann Lordeman

SUMMARY

The Individuals with Disabilities Education Act (IDEA) is both a grants statute and a civil rights statute. As a grants statute, IDEA provides federal funding for the education of children with disabilities and requires, as a condition for the receipt of such funds, the provision of a free appropriate public education (FAPE) (i.e., specially designed instruction provided at no cost to parents that meets the needs of a child with a disability). In FY2012, $12.6 billion was appropriated for IDEA. In the fall of 2009, 5.9 million children ages six through 21 received educational services under IDEA.

As a civil rights statute, IDEA contains procedural safeguards, which are provisions intended to protect the rights of parents and children with disabilities regarding the provision of FAPE. These procedures include parental rights to resolve disputes through a mediation process, and present and resolve complaints through a due process complaint

---

* This is an edited, reformatted and augmented version of Congressional Research Service, Publication No. R41833, dated January 7, 2013.

procedure, and through state complaint procedures. IDEA's procedural safeguards also address disciplinary issues. In general, a child with a disability is not immune from discipline, but the procedures are not the same as for non-disabled children.

To be covered under IDEA, a child with a disability must meet the categorical definition of disability in the act, and the child must require special education and related services as a result of the disability in order to benefit from public education. Once a child meets IDEA's eligibility criteria, FAPE is implemented through the Individualized Education Program (IEP), which is the plan for providing special education and related services by the local educational agency (LEA). The IEP is developed by an IEP team composed of school personnel and parents. IDEA requires that children with disabilities be educated in the least restrictive environment. That is, to the maximum extent appropriate they are to be educated with children who are not disabled. In 2008, over 50% of all children with disabilities served by IDEA spent 80% or more of their time in a regular classroom.

To implement IDEA, states and other entities (i.e., the District of Columbia, Puerto Rico, the Bureau of Indian Education, the outlying areas, and the freely associated states) receive grants based on a statutory formula. Most of the federal funds received by states are passed on to LEAs based on a statutory formula. IDEA also contains state and local maintenance of effort (MOE) requirements and supplement, not supplant (SNS) requirements aimed at increasing overall educational spending, rather than substituting federal funds for education spending at the state and local levels.

Originally enacted in 1975, IDEA has been the subject of numerous reauthorizations to extend services and rights to children with disabilities. The most recent reauthorization of IDEA was P.L. 108-446 enacted in 2004. Funding for Part B, Assistance for Education of all Children with Disabilities, the largest and most often discussed part of the act, is permanently authorized. Funding for Part C, Infants and Toddlers with Disabilities, and Part D, National Activities, was authorized through FY2011. Funding for the programs continues to be authorized through annual appropriations.

INTRODUCTION

Background

The Individuals with Disabilities Education Act (IDEA) is the main federal statute governing special education for children from birth through age

21.[1] IDEA protects the rights of children with disabilities to a free appropriate public education (FAPE). It also supplements state and local funding to pay for some of the additional or excess costs of educating children with disabilities. IDEA is administered by the Office of Special Education Programs (OSEP) in the Office of Special Education and Rehabilitative Services (OSERS) in the Department of Education (ED). In the fall of 2008, a total of 6.6 million public school students age six though 21 were served by IDEA Part B, representing approximately 13% of all public school students in this age range.[2]

IDEA was originally enacted in 1975 as the Education for All Handicapped Children Act, P.L. 94- 142.[3] At that time, Congress found that more than half of all children with disabilities were not receiving appropriate educational services and that 1 million children with disabilities were excluded entirely from the public school system. Further, Congress found that many of the children participating in regular school programs were prevented from having a successful educational experience because their disabilities were undiagnosed.[4] In addition to the awareness of the difficulties faced by children with disabilities, there were three other factors that precipitated the enactment of P.L. 94-142: (1) judicial decisions that found constitutional requirements for the education of children with disabilities, (2) the inability of states and localities to fund education for children with disabilities, and (3) potential long-term benefits of educating children with disabilities.[5]

IDEA consists of four parts. Part A contains the general provisions, including the purposes of the act and definitions. Part B contains provisions relating to the education of school aged children (the grants-to-states program) and state grants program for preschool children with disabilities (Section 619). Part C authorizes state grants for programs serving infants and toddlers with disabilities, while Part D contains the requirements for various national activities designed to improve the education of children with disabilities. Table 1 shows the structure and funding of IDEA. Appendix A provides a more detailed summary of each of the four parts.

Since 1975, IDEA has been the subject of numerous reauthorizations to extend services and rights to children with disabilities. The most recent reauthorization was P.L. 108-446 in 2004.[6] Funding for Part B, Assistance for Education of all Children with Disabilities, is permanently authorized. Funding for Part C, Infants and Toddlers with Disabilities, and Part D, National Activities, was authorized through FY2011.[7]

Table 1. Structure and Funding of IDEA (funding in thousands of dollars)

IDEA Part	Description	FY2012 Funding	Percentage of Total IDEA Funding
Part A—General Provisions	Includes findings, purposes, and definitions	—	—
Part B—Assistance for Education of all Children with Disabilities	Contains provisions relating to the education of school aged children (the grants-to-states program) and state grants program for preschool children with disabilities (Section 619)	$11,950,501[a]	94.5%
Part C—Infants and Toddlers with Disabilities	Authorizes state grants for programs serving infants and toddlers with disabilities	$442,710	3.5%
Part D—National Activities to Improve Education of Children with Disabilities	Contains the requirements for various national activities	$247,498	2.0%
IDEA Total		$12,640,709	100%

Source: Table prepared by CRS. Funding amounts are from Department of Education budget tables for FY2012, and reflect the 0.189 percent rescission required by P.L. 112-74.

a. Of this amount, $372.6 million, or 3% of the total IDEA FY2012 appropriation, was appropriated for the state grants program for preschool children with disabilities (Section 619).

Three of the main purposes of IDEA are

> (A) to ensure that all children with disabilities have available to them a free appropriate public education that emphasizes special education and related services designed to meet their unique needs and prepare them for further education, employment, and independent living; (B) to ensure that the rights of children with disabilities and parents of such children are protected; and (C) to assist states, localities, educational service agencies, and Federal agencies to provide for the education of all children with disabilities;[8]

The focus of this report will be on how these purposes are to be achieved under Part B of IDEA, hereafter referred to as IDEA. The first purpose is addressed primarily in the section of this report titled "Services for Children with Disabilities." The second is addressed in the section on "Procedural

Safeguards," and the third is addressed in the section on "Funding, Expenditure Requirements, and Compliance."

SERVICES FOR CHILDREN WITH DISABILITIES

Children with disabilities receive specially designed instruction and other services to meet their unique needs. This section addresses (1) criteria children must meet to receive services under IDEA, (2) how the children are identified and evaluated, and (3) the procedures for developing an individualized plan to provide special education and related services.

Categories of Disabilities
Autism Deaf-blindness Deafness Emotional disturbance Hearing impairment Mental retardation Multiple disabilities Orthopedic impairment Other health impairment Specific learning disability Speech or language impairment Traumatic brain injury Visual impairment

Children with Disabilities

To be covered under IDEA, a child with a disability must meet two criteria. First, the child must be in one of several categories of disabilities, and second, the child must require special education and related services as a result of the disability in order to benefit from public education.[9] If a child meets the two criteria, he or she would be eligible to receive specially designed instruction or special education in which the content or the delivery of the instruction is adapted to the needs of the child. If a child has a disability, but does not require special education to benefit from public education, he or she would not be covered under IDEA. The child might be covered, however, under two other acts that address the rights of individuals with disabilities: Section 504 of the Rehabilitation Act[10] or the Americans with Disabilities Act (ADA).[11] These two acts provide broad nondiscrimination protection not limited to education and have identical functional definitions of disability (i.e., disabilities related to such functions as seeing, hearing, walking, thinking) rather than the categorical definition of IDEA. "Several of the most common disabilities of students included under Section 504 and the ADA, but not always covered under IDEA, are attention deficit hyperactivity disorder (ADHD), diabetes, and asthma."[12]

Figure 1 shows the distribution of students with disabilities age six through 21 receiving special education and related services in the fall of 2009. Forty-two percent of students with disabilities have specific learning disabilities (SLD).[13] Learning disabilities include such conditions as perceptual disabilities, brain injury, minimal brain dysfunction, dyslexia, and developmental aphasia.[14]

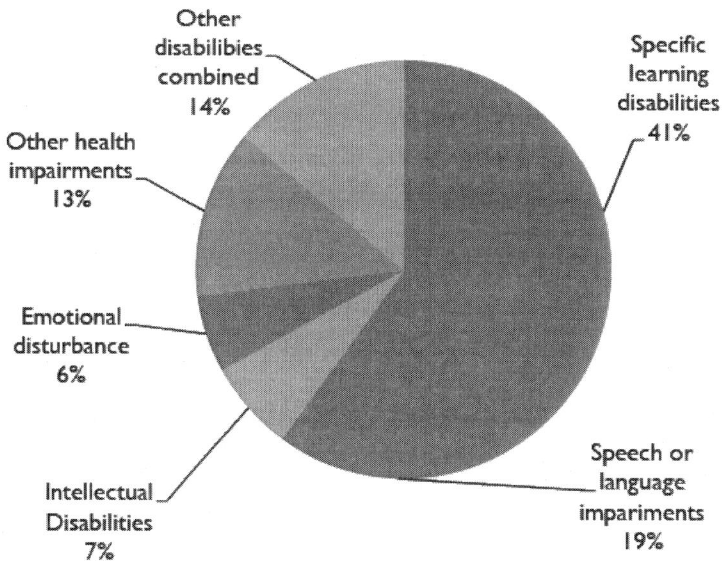

Source: Data Accountability Center, Part B Child Count (2011), MS-EXCEL Table B1-3, https://www.ideadata.org/arc_toc13.asp#partbCC.

Notes: Percentages may not add to 100% because of rounding. Total number of students is 5.8 million.

Other disabilities combined include multiple disabilities, hearing impairments, orthopedic impairments, visual impairments, autism, deaf-blindness, traumatic brain injury, and developmental delay.

Figure 1. Disability Distribution for Students ages six through 21 Receiving Special Education and Related Services under IDEA, Part B: Fall 2011.

Free Appropriate Public Education (FAPE)

All children with disabilities between the ages of three and 21, inclusive, residing in a state are entitled to FAPE.[15] The term "free appropriate public education" means

> special education and related services that—(A) have been provided at public expense, under public supervision and direction, and without charge; (B) meet the standards of the state educational agency; (C) include an appropriate preschool, elementary school, or secondary school education in the state involved; and (D) are provided in conformity with the individualized education program required under section 614(d) [Individualized Education Programs (IEP)].[16]

In addition, FAPE must be available to a child with a disability who has been suspended or expelled from school.[17] FAPE must also be available to a child with a disability who needs special education and related services even though the child has not failed or been retained in a course or grade and is advancing from grade to grade.[18]

Identification and Evaluation

Identifying and Evaluating a Child with a Disability

The first step in providing FAPE to children with disabilities is identifying them. Each state must have in effect policies and procedures to ensure that all children with disabilities residing in the state who are in need of special education and related services are identified, located, and evaluated. These policies and procedures are referred to in statute as "child find."[19] The children include those with disabilities who are

- homeless or wards of the state,
- attending private schools,
- suspected of having a disability, and
- highly mobile children, including migrant children.

A child who has been identified as having (or possibly having) a disability must be evaluated by the LEA before receiving special education and related services to determine whether a child is a child with a disability and to determine the educational needs of the child.[20] Either the parent or the LEA may request an initial evaluation.[21] In general, the LEA must obtain informed consent from the parent before conducting an initial evaluation.[22] Parental consent for an evaluation cannot be construed as consent for special education and related services.[23] The initial evaluation must take place within 60 days of receiving parental consent or within an alternative time frame established by the state.[24]

In conducting the initial evaluation, the LEA must

- use a variety of assessment tools and strategies to gather relevant functional, developmental, and academic information, including information provided by the parent;
- not use any single measure or assessment as the sole criterion for determining whether a child is a child with a disability or determining an appropriate educational program for the child; and
- use technically sound instruments that may assess the relative contribution of cognitive and behavioral factors, in addition to physical or developmental factors.[25]

In addition, assessments and other evaluation materials used to assess a child must be selected and administered so as not to be discriminatory on a racial or cultural basis. They must also be provided and administered in the language and form most likely to yield accurate information on what the child knows and can do academically, developmentally, and functionally.[26]

Upon completion of the evaluation, the determination of whether the child is a child with a disability is made and the educational needs of the child are decided by a team of qualified professionals and by the parent of the child.[27] A copy of the evaluation report and the documentation of determination of eligibility is given to the parent.[28] In making a determination of eligibility, a child shall not be determined to be a child with a disability if the determinant factor is lack of appropriate instruction in reading, lack of instruction in math, or limited English proficiency.[29]

Reevaluations are required if the child's teacher or parent makes a request or if the LEA determines that the child's educational and service needs, academic achievement, or functional performance warrant a reevaluation. For example, a reevaluation might be warranted if the child's performance in school significantly improves, suggesting that he or she no longer requires special education and related services, or if the child is not making progress toward the goals in his or her IEP, indicating that changes are needed in the education or related services the LEA is providing. A reevaluation may not be done more than once a year unless the parent and LEA agree, and must be done at least once every three years unless the parent and the LEA agree that a reevaluation is not necessary.[30] In general, parental consent is required for reevaluations as well as for the initial evaluation.[31] In addition, the LEA cannot change the eligibility of a child until a reevaluation is done, unless the child graduates from high school with a regular diploma or reaches the age at which state law no longer provides for FAPE.[32]

Identifying and Evaluating a Child with a Specific Learning Disability (SLD)

As noted above, 43% of children with disabilities have SLDs. It is therefore worth noting the procedures required for identifying a child with an SLD. In addition to the procedures addressed above for identifying a child with a disability, the statute and regulations allow additional procedures.[33] In general, a state must adopt criteria for determining whether a child has an SLD, and an LEA must use the state criteria.[34] The state criteria cannot require the use of a severe discrepancy between intellectual ability and achievement for determining whether a child has a specific learning disability;[35] must permit the use of a process based on the child's response to scientific, research-based intervention;[36] and may permit the use of other alternative research-based procedures for determining whether a child has an SLD.[37]

In general, the group members who determine whether a child has an SLD must include the child's parents, the child's regular education teacher, and at least one person qualified to conduct individual diagnostic examinations of children (e.g., a school psychologist, speech-language pathologist, or remedial reading teacher).[38] The group may determine that a child has an SLD if three criteria are met:[39]

- The child does not achieve adequately for the child's age or meet state-approved grade-level standards in one or more of eight areas[40] when provided with learning experiences and instruction appropriate for the child's age or state-approved grade-level standards.
- The child either does not make sufficient progress to meet age or state-approved grade-level standards in one or more of the eight areas when using a process based on the child's response to scientific, research-based intervention; or the child exhibits a pattern of strengths and weaknesses in performance, achievement, or both, relative to age, state-approved grade-level standards, or intellectual development that

is determined by the group to be relevant to the identification of an SLD.

- If the child is found to have an SLD, it is not primarily the result of a visual, hearing, or motor disability; mental retardation; emotional disturbance; cultural factors; environmental or economic disadvantage; or limited English proficiency.

To ensure that underachievement in a child suspected of having an SLD is not due to lack of appropriate instruction in reading or math, the group must consider, as part of the evaluation, (1) data that demonstrate that prior to, or as a part of, the referral process, the child was provided appropriate instruction in regular education settings, delivered by qualified personnel; and (2) data-based documentation of repeated assessments of achievement at reasonable intervals, reflecting formal assessment of student progress during instruction, which was provided to the child's parents.[41]

If prior to a referral for an evaluation, a child has not made adequate progress after an appropriate period of time when provided instruction, an LEA must promptly request parental consent to evaluate the child.[42] The regulations also specify that the child must be observed in the child's learning environment to document the child's academic performance and behavior in the areas of difficulty.[43] Finally, the regulations detail the specific documentation for determining eligibility for a child suspected of having an SLD.[44]

The Individualized Education Program (IEP)

FAPE is implemented through the IEP, which is the plan for providing special education and related services by the LEA to the child with a disability. It is developed by an IEP team composed of school personnel and parents. In general, the IEP team must consider the strengths of the child; the concerns of the parents for enhancing the education of their child; the results of the initial evaluation (or most recent evaluation); and the academic, developmental, and functional needs of the child.[45] The IEP team meets at least once a year to review the IEP to determine if goals are being met and to make necessary changes.[46] The team must meet to develop the initial IEP for a child within 30 days of determining that the child needs special education and related services. In addition, as soon as possible following the development of the IEP, special education and related services must be made available to the child in accordance with the IEP.[47]

Content of IEP[48]

Specifically, IDEA requires that the IEP include the following:

- the child's present levels of academic achievement and functional performance;
- measurable annual goals, including academic and functional goals, designed to
  - meet the child's needs that result from the child's disability to enable the child to be involved in and make progress in the general education curriculum; and
  - meet each of the child's other educational needs that result from the child's disability;
- how the child's progress toward meeting the above annual goals will be measured and when periodic reports on the progress the child is making toward meeting the annual goals will be provided;
- the special education and related services and supplementary aids and services, based on peer-reviewed research to the extent practicable, to be provided to the child, or on behalf of the child, and the program modifications or supports for school personnel that will be provided for the child to
  - advance appropriately toward attaining the annual goals;
  - be involved in and make progress in the general education curriculum and participate in extracurricular and other nonacademic activities; and
  - be educated and participate with other children with disabilities and nondisabled children;
- the extent, if any, to which the child will not participate with nondisabled children in the regular class;
- any individual appropriate accommodations[49] that are necessary to measure the academic achievement and functional performance of the child on state and district-wide assessments; if the IEP team determines that the child will take an alternate assessment on a particular state or district-wide assessment of student achievement, the IEP should detail why the child cannot participate in the regular assessment and why the particular alternate assessment selected is appropriate for the child;[50]

- the projected date for the beginning of the assessments and their frequency, location, and duration.

In addition, beginning not later than when the first IEP is in effect when the child is 16, and updated annually thereafter, the IEP must include appropriate measurable postsecondary goals related to training, education, employment, and, where appropriate, independent living skills and the transition services[51] needed to assist the child in reaching those goals.

The IEP Team[52]

Each child identified as a child with a disability must have an IEP developed by an IEP team. In general, the composition of the team includes

- the parents of a child with a disability;
- one or more regular education teachers, if the child is or may be participating in the regular education environment;
- one or more special education teachers;
- a representative of the LEA who is qualified to provide or supervise the provision of special education; is knowledgeable about the general education curriculum; and is knowledgeable about the availability of resources of the LEA;
- an individual who can interpret the instructional implications of evaluation results;
- at the discretion of the parent or the agency, other individuals who have knowledge or special expertise regarding the child, including related services personnel, as appropriate; and
- whenever appropriate, the child with a disability.[53]

Special Education and Related Services

The provision of special education and related services is a key component of FAPE. Special education means "specially designed instruction, at no cost to parents, to meet the unique needs of a child with a disability, including—(A) instruction conducted in the classroom, in the home, in hospitals and institutions, and in other settings; and (B) instruction in physical education."[54] Specially designed instruction, which is delineated in the IEP, means that the content, methodology, or delivery of instruction is adapted to address the unique needs of the child that result from the child's disability. The instruction must ensure the child's access to the general curriculum, so that the child can meet the educational standards that apply to all children. While specially designed instruction is provided at no cost to parents, parents can be required to pay any incidental fees that are normally charged to nondisabled students or their parents as a part of the regular education program.[55]

In general, related services are transportation and those developmental, corrective, and other supportive services required to help a child with a disability to benefit from special education. Both the statute and federal regulations define related services and provide a list of related services.[56] The regulations also further define the services that may be provided to a child with a disability. The list is not exhaustive; other related services could be provided to a child with a disability. Related services include the following:

- speech-language pathology and audiology services;
- interpreting services for children who are deaf, hard of hearing, or deaf-blind;
- psychological services;
- physical therapy and occupation therapy;
- recreation, including therapeutic recreation;
- social work services in schools;
- school health services and school nurse services;
- counseling services, including rehabilitation counseling;
- orientation and mobility services provided to blind or visually impaired children;
- parent counseling and training;
- medical services for diagnostic and evaluation purposes only;[57] and
- early identification and assessment of disabilities through the implementation of a formal plan for identifying a disability.

Coordinated Early Intervening Services (CEIS)

With some restrictions, LEAs may use up to 15% of their allocations[58] "to develop and implement coordinated, early intervening services, which may include interagency financing structures, for students in kindergarten through grade 12 (with a particular emphasis on students in kindergarten through grade 3) who have not been identified as needing special education or related services but who need additional academic and behavioral support to succeed in a general education environment."[59] CEIS may not, however, delay an appropriate evaluation of a child suspected of having a disability.[60]

In its analysis of comments and changes to the final regulations, ED discusses the potential benefits of CEIS as follows:

> The authority to use some Part B funds for early intervening services has the potential to benefit special education, as well as the education of other children, by reducing academic and behavioral problems in the regular educational environment and reducing the number of referrals to special education that could have been avoided by relatively simple regular education interventions.[61]

LEAs may use CEIS funds for both professional development for teachers and other school staff and for educational and behavioral evaluations, services, and supports to students.[62] Funds may also be used to carry out CEIS that are aligned with activities funded by, and carried out under, the Elementary and Secondary Education Act of 1965 (ESEA) if the funds supplement, and do not supplant, ESEA funds.[63]

A state must require an LEA to use up to 15% of its funds for CEIS if the state has determined through statutorily required data collection that "significant disproportionality"[64] based on race and ethnicity is occurring with respect to the identification of children with disabilities; their placement in particular education settings; and the incidence, duration, and type of disciplinary actions, including suspensions and expulsions.[65] The funds are to be used to provide CEIS "to serve children in the LEA, particularly, but not exclusively, children in those groups that were significantly overidentified."[66]

Response to Intervention (RTI)

One way that coordinated early intervening services are provided is through an approach called Response to Intervention (RTI). RTI "is a multi-level framework to maximize student achievement by providing support to students at risk for poor learning outcomes."[67] While there are many models of RTI, ED notes that

> the core characteristics that underpin all RTI models are: (1) students receive high quality research-based instruction in their general education setting; (2) continuous monitoring of student performance; (3) all students are screened for academic and behavioral problems; and (4) multiple levels (tiers) of instruction that are progressively more intense, based on the student's response to instruction.

For example, an RTI model with a three-tier continuum of school-wide support might include the following tiers and levels of support: (1) Tier one (Primary Intervention), for all students using high quality scientific research-based instruction in their general education setting. It would not be appropriate to use EIS funds for these activities since these students do not need additional academic and behavioral support to succeed in a general education environment. (2) Tier two (Secondary Intervention), for specialized small group instruction of students determined to be at risk for academic and behavioral problems. It would be appropriate to use EIS funds to support these activities. (3) Tier three (Tertiary Intervention) for specialized individualized instructional /behavioral support for students with intensive needs. EIS funds could not be used if these students were currently receiving special education or related services.[68]

Highly Qualified Teachers

Each SEA must ensure that each special education teacher who teaches elementary or secondary school is "highly qualified."[69] The term "highly qualified" as defined in IDEA is linked to the definition in ESEA. In brief, ESEA requires that public school teachers of "core academic subjects"[70] obtain full state teaching certification or pass the state teacher licensing examination, or fulfill requirements in a state's charter school law for teachers in charter schools; have not had any certification requirements waived on an emergency, temporary, or provisional basis; and have a bachelor's degree.[71] IDEA modifies the ESEA definition as it applies to special education teachers.[72] IDEA requires that *all special education teachers*, whether they teach core academic subjects or not, obtain full state *special education* teaching certification or pass the state teacher licensing examination, or fulfill requirements in a state's charter school law for teachers in charter schools; have not had any certification requirements waived on an emergency, temporary, or provisional basis; and have a bachelor's degree. In addition, IDEA has specific provisions related to teachers who teach only the most severely disabled children and those who teach more than one core subject.[73]

The Educational Environment

IDEA requires that children with disabilities be educated in the least restrictive environment possible.[74] In other words, to the maximum extent that is appropriate they are to be educated with children who are not disabled. Further, special classes, separate schooling, or other removal of children with disabilities from the regular educational environment can occur only when the nature or severity of the disability of a child is such that education in regular classes with the use of supplementary aids and services[75] cannot be achieved satisfactorily. Supplementary aids and services could include such things as additional time to take tests or complete assignments, slower-paced instruction, personal aides, peer tutors, and use of a computer.

The LEA must also ensure that there is a continuum of alternate placements that includes instruction in regular classes, special classes, special schools, home instruction, and instruction in hospitals and institutions. This continuum must also make provision for supplementary services to be provided in conjunction with regular class placement.[76]

The specific placement decision for each child with a disability must be made by a group of persons, including the parents, and other persons knowledgeable about the child, the meaning of the evaluation data, and placement options.

The child's placement must be (1) determined at least annually, (2) based on the IEP, and (3) as close to home as possible.[77]

As with identification and evaluation, the child's parents must be notified in writing within a reasonable time before the placement.[78] If the parents disagree with the placement decision, they may use the procedural safeguards, such as the mediation and due process complaints discussed in the "Procedural Safeguards " section of this report.

As shown in Table 2, which contains the most recent data available, 58% of children with disabilities age 6-21 spend 80% or more of their time in the regular classroom; 21% spend between 40% and 79%; 15% spend less than 40%; and 5% are educated in other environments. Other environments are a separate school, a residential facility, a private school placement by the parent, a correctional facility, and a home or hospital.

Only 3% of all children with disabilities ages six through 21 receive their education in a separate school and an additional 1% are parentally placed in a private school. As also shown in Table 2, 62% of children with SLDs and 87% with speech and language impairments spend 80% or more their classroom time in the regular classroom, while only 17% of children with mental retardation spend 80% or more of their time in the regular classroom.

Table 2. Percentage of Time Students Ages six through 21 Spend in a Regular Classroom and in Other Environments, under IDEA Part B: Fall 2008

Disability	Percentage Who Spend 80% or More of Time in a Regular Classroom	Percentage Who Spend 40%-79% of Time in a Regular Classroom	Percentage Who Spend Less than 40% of Time in a Regular Classroom	Percentage Who Spend Time in an Environment Other than a Regular Classroom
All disabilities	58%	21%	15%	5%
Specific learning disability	62%	28%	8%	2%
Speech or language impairments	87%	6%	5%	3%
Mental retardation	17%	27%	48%	8%
Emotional disturbance	39%	19%	23%	18%
Other health impairments	60%	24%	11%	4%

Source: Data Accountability Center, Part B Educational Environment (2008), MS-EXCEL Table 2-2, https://www.ideadata.org/arc_toc10.asp#partbLRE.

Notes: Percentages by disability may not add to 100% because of rounding. Total number of students is 5.9 million.

Children with Disabilities in Private Schools[79]

A child with a disability may be placed in a private elementary or secondary school by an LEA as part of an IEP if the IEP team determines that a private school placement is needed to fulfill the FAPE requirements for the child. In this situation, the private school placement is made at no cost to the parents, and the child has all of the rights of a child with a disability who is served in a public school.[80]

A child with a disability may also be unilaterally placed in a private elementary or secondary school by his or her parents.[81] In this situation, the "parentally placed" child is not entitled to FAPE, and the cost of the private school placement is not paid by the LEA unless a court or hearing officer makes certain findings.[82]

The LEA must, however, spend a share of its IDEA funds to provide services to children enrolled with disabilities by their parents in private schools located in the LEA based on the proportion of parentally placed children to the total number of children with disabilities in the LEA.[83] Except where there is a court order, the LEA makes the final decision about the services to be provided to parentally placed private school children.[84]

In making this decision, the LEA must engage in a consultation process with the private school officials and representatives of parents.[85] The LEA is also responsible for devising a service plan for every parentally placed child with a disability receiving special education or related services from the LEA.[86]

PROCEDURAL SAFEGUARDS

Procedural safeguards[87] are provisions protecting the rights of parents and children with disabilities regarding FAPE. The various types of procedures include parental rights to

- inspect and review educational records;[88]
- participate in meetings related to the identification, evaluation, and educational placement of their child;[89]
- obtain an independent educational evaluation at public expense if the parent disagrees with an evaluation obtained by the LEA;[90]
- receive prior written notice in the native language of the parents when an LEA proposes to initiate or change, or refuses to initiate or change, the identification, evaluation, or educational placement of the child or the provision of FAPE to the child;[91]
- receive a procedural safeguards notice, which is a comprehensive written explanation of IDEA's legal rights and protections for children with disabilities and their parents;[92]
- resolve disputes through a mediation process;[93]
- present and resolve complaints through the due process complaint procedures, which include a right to file suit in federal district court;[94] and
- present and resolve complaints through state complaint procedures.[95]

Three of the procedural safeguards listed above pertain to dispute resolution between parents and the LEA. These are mediation, due process complaint procedures, and state complaint procedures, which are discussed below. IDEA's disciplinary provisions, discussed in this section as well, also include procedural safeguards to protect the rights of children with disabilities to FAPE.

Mediation[96]

Mediation is a process of resolving disputes initiated by either the parent or LEA involving any matter under IDEA. It is a way of resolving complaints without a formal due process hearing, discussed below. Either a parent or an LEA can initiate the mediation process, which must be voluntary for each party. The mediation must be conducted by a qualified and impartial mediator who is trained in effective mediation techniques. The cost of the mediation process is borne by the state.

If the school and parent resolve a dispute through the mediation process, they must execute a legally binding agreement that is signed by the parent and a representative of the LEA. This agreement is enforceable in state or U.S. district court. Discussions that occur during the mediation process must be confidential and may not be used in any subsequent due process hearing or civil proceeding of any federal or state court.

Due Process Complaint Procedures

The due process complaint procedure begins with filing a due process complaint, which is in effect a request for a due process hearing, on matters relating to the identification, evaluation, or educational placement of a child with a disability, or the provision of FAPE to the child.

Generally, unless the SEA or LEA and the parent otherwise agree, the child must remain in his or her current educational placement pending the outcome of the due process complaint procedures or of a court proceeding. This requirement is referred to as "stay put."[97]

Either a parent or an LEA may file a due process complaint.[98] The due process complaint must allege a violation that occurred not more than two years before the date the parent or public agency knew or should have known about the alleged action that forms the basis of the due process complaint, or, if the state has an explicit time limitation for filing a due process complaint, occurred in the time period allowed by state law.[99]

Within 15 days of receiving the due process complaint, the LEA must convene a resolution session to attempt to resolve the issues unless the parents and LEA agree to waive the session. If the issues are not resolved, the due process hearing may occur. If the complaint is not resolved through mediation, a resolution meeting, or a due process hearing, either party to the complaint can file a civil suit.[100]

The due process hearing is conducted by an impartial hearing officer.[101] The decision of the hearing officer is final, except that any party in a state where the hearing is conducted by the LEA may appeal the findings and decision to the SEA, who in turn must conduct an impartial review. If the hearing was held in a state where the SEA conducted the hearing, then either party can file a civil lawsuit. The party filing the lawsuit has 90 days from the date of the decision of the hearing officer or, if applicable, the decision of the state review official, to file the lawsuit; or, if the state has an explicit time limitation for bringing civil action, the lawsuit must be filed in the time period allowed by state law.[102]

State Complaint Procedures[103]

The IDEA regulations require each state to adopt written procedures for resolving complaints that allege LEA violations of the statute or regulations. In its analysis of comments and changes to the final regulations, ED distinguishes between the due process complaint process and the state complaint process as follows:

> The due process complaint procedures and the State complaint procedures are separate and distinct. The State complaint procedures remain a viable alternative to the due process procedures for parents to resolve disputes with public agencies in a less formal and more cost effective manner.[104]

Unlike requests for mediation or for complaints filed under due process procedures, where only a parent or an LEA can file a complaint, a state complaint can be filed by any organization or individual, including those from another state. State complaint procedures must ensure that complaints will be resolved within 60 calendar days from the date the complaint is filed unless an extension is permitted.[105]

Discipline[106]

IDEA's disciplinary provisions are intended to "balance school safety issues with the need to ensure that schools respond appropriately to a child's behavior that was caused by, or directly and substantially related to, the child's disability."[107] IDEA addresses both the school's authority in disciplining students with disabilities and the rights of the students to receive FAPE. In general, a child with a disability is not immune from disciplinary procedures; however, these procedures are not identical to those for children without disabilities.[108]

If a child with a disability commits an action that would be subject to discipline, school personnel have several immediate options. These include

- removing a child from his or her current placement to another setting or suspension for up to 10 school days;[109]
- placing the child in an interim alternative education setting for up to 45 school days for situations involving weapons or drugs, or if the student has inflicted serious bodily injury on another person while at school;[110] and
- asking a hearing officer to order a child to be placed in an interim alternative educational setting for up to 45 school days if the hearing officer determines that maintaining the current placement of the child is substantially likely to result in injury to the child or others.[111]

If an LEA seeks to change the placement of a child with a disability for more than 10 days, the LEA must first determine

> (I) if the conduct in question was caused by, or had a direct and substantial relationship to, the child's disability; or (II) if the conduct in question was the direct result of the local educational agency's failure to implement the IEP.[112]

This determination is referred to as a "manifestation determination." The reason for the determination is IDEA's recognition "that a child with a disability may display disruptive behaviors characteristic of the child's disability and the child should not be punished for behaviors that are a result of the child's disability."[113]

If the child's behavior is not a manifestation of a disability, long-term disciplinary action such as expulsion may occur, except that educational services may not cease.[114] If the behavior is a manifestation of the disability, the IEP team must conduct a functional behavior assessment and implement a behavior intervention plan for the child, if this has not been done before.[115] If there was a behavioral intervention plan, it must be reviewed and modified as necessary to address the behavior.[116]

Except for certain circumstances involving weapons, illegal drugs, or serious bodily injury, when the conduct is a manifestation of the disability, the child must return to the placement from which he or she was removed unless the parent and the LEA agree to a change of placement as part of the modification of the behavioral intervention plan.[117] If the parent of a child with a disability disagrees with any decision regarding placement or the manifestation determination, or an LEA believes that maintaining the current placement of the child is substantially likely to result in injury to the child or others, either may request a due process hearing.[118]

Nothing in IDEA is to be construed as prohibiting an LEA from reporting a crime committed by a child with a disability to the appropriate authorities. An LEA reporting a crime committed by a child with a disability will ensure that copies of the special education and disciplinary records of the child are transmitted for consideration by the appropriate authorities to whom the agency reports the crime.[119]

Funding, Expenditure Requirements, and Compliance

IDEA provides federal funding for the education of children with disabilities and imposes certain conditions for the receipt of federal funds. This section addresses state and local (1) funding allocations; (2) expenditure requirements, including maintenance of effort provisions; and (3) compliance with IDEA provisions through federal and state monitoring and enforcement requirements.

Funding

Actual and proposed grants to states are often discussed in terms of the percent of the "excess costs" of educating children with disabilities that the federal government will pay.[120] The metric for determining this excess cost is based on the national average per-pupil expenditure (APPE). In 1975, with the enactment of the Education for All Handicapped Children Act (P.L. 94-142), it was determined that the federal government would pay up to 40% of this excess cost.[121] This 40% of the excess cost is often referred to as "full funding." For FY2012, the Part B grants to states appropriation of $11.6 billion provides an estimated percentage of APPE of 16%.[122]

State Formula Allocations

Of the funds appropriated for IDEA, the Secretary of Education first reserves (1) not more than 1% of the appropriation for the outlying areas and freely associated states,[123] (2) funds for services for Indian children with disabilities,[124] and (3) not more than one-half of 1% of the appropriation up to a maximum of $25 million, adjusted for inflation, to provide technical assistance to improve the capacity of states to meet data collection requirements.[125] The remainder of the funds are allocated by a formula to the 50 states, the District of Columbia, and Puerto Rico. If the amount available for allocations to states for a fiscal year is equal to or greater than the amount allocated to the states for the preceding fiscal year, the formula[126] first requires that each state receive a base grant, which is the amount received by the state for FY1999. The next step is to distribute 85% of the remaining funds among the states based on states' shares of total population ages three to 21[127] and 15% of the remaining funds based on states' shares of poor children in that age range. The third step ensures that states do not receive less than certain minimum amounts or more than certain maximum amounts.[128] If the amount available for allocation to states decreases from the prior year, any amount available for allocation to states above the 1999 level is allocated based on the relative increases in funding that the states received between 1999 and the prior year. If there is a decrease below the amount allocated for 1999, each state's allocation is ratably reduced from the 1999 level.[129]

State-Level Activities

A state may reserve funds from their grants for administration[130] and for a variety of other statewide activities. These include two mandatory activities: (1) monitoring, enforcement, and complaint investigation, and (2) establishing and maintaining a parental mediation process.[131] Other allowable state-level activities include improving the use of technology in the classroom, developing transition programs, and assisting LEAs in meeting personnel shortages.[132] In addition, for the purpose of assisting LEAs in addressing the needs of high-need children (i.e., children who require expensive services, including certain medical expenses), states may establish a risk pool or "high cost" fund. If a state chooses to establish a risk pool, it must use 10% of the funds it reserved for state-level activities.[133] States using a risk pool must develop and annually review a state plan in which the state determines which children with disabilities are high need, set out the procedures by which LEAs participate in the risk pool, and determine how funds are distributed.[134] Funds distributed from the risk pool must only pay for "direct special education and related services" for high need children with disabilities[135] and may not be used for legal fees or related costs.[136] If some funds reserved for the risk pool are not distributed for services for high-need children, they are to be distributed to LEAs according to the substate formula.[137]

LEA Formula Allocations

Funds remaining after funds for state-level activities are set aside are distributed to LEAs based on a formula similar to the state formula. Like the state formula, LEAs are first allocated base grants. Also similar to the state formula, 85% of the remaining funds is allocated based on LEAs' shares of public and private school enrollment and 15% of the remaining funds is allocated based on shares of children living in poverty, as determined by the SEA. There is no minimum or maximum grant.[138]

State and LEA Expenditure Requirements

IDEA state and LEA expenditure requirements are aimed at increasing overall educational spending, rather than substituting federal funds for education spending at the state and local levels. Maintenance of effort (MOE) provisions basically require that a state or an LEA not reduce its support for special education and related services below the level of support it provided the previous fiscal year. Supplement, not supplant (SNS) requirements generally prohibit a state or LEA from using IDEA grants to provide services, purchase equipment, etc., that state, local, or other federal funds currently provide or purchase or, in the absence of the IDEA funds, that those other funds would have provided or would have purchased.

Maintenance of Effort (MOE)

In general, a state may not reduce the amount of its financial support for special education and related services for children with disabilities below the amount of that support for the preceding fiscal year.[139] In any fiscal year in which a state does not meet this MOE requirement, the Secretary of Education is required to reduce the state's subsequent year grant by the same amount by which the state fails to meet the requirement.[140] The Secretary may grant a waiver for one fiscal year at a time in the case of "exceptional or uncontrollable circumstances" such as a natural disaster or a "precipitous and unforeseen decline in the financial resources of the state."[141] In addition, waivers can be granted if the state can provide "clear and convincing evidence" that FAPE is available for all children with disabilities.[142] If a state does not meet its MOE requirement for any year, including any year for which the state was granted a waiver, the state financial support required in future years is not reduced. That is, the state must provide the amount that would have been required in the absence of failing to meet MOE in the previous year.[143]

LEAs may use IDEA funds only for the excess costs[144] of educating children with disabilities, and may not reduce the level of expenditures for the education of children with disabilities made by the LEA from local funds below the level of those expenditures for the preceding fiscal year.[145] In general, the SEA must determine that an LEA meets this requirement (for purposes of establishing the LEA's eligibility for an award for a fiscal year). If the LEA assures the SEA that it will provide at least the same total or per capita amount from either local funds only or a combination of state and local funds for the most recent prior year for which the data are available, then the LEA would be eligible for funds.[146] IDEA specifies in statute four circumstances in which an LEA may legally reduce its local expenditures. These are in cases of

> (1) voluntary departure, by retirement or otherwise, or departure for just cause, of special education personnel; (2) a decrease in the enrollment of children with disabilities; (3) the termination of the obligation of the agency ... to provide a program of special education to a particular child with a disability that is an exceptionally costly program ... ; or (4) the termination of costly expenditures for long-term purchases, such as the acquisition of equipment or the construction of school facilities.[147]

The regulations establish a fifth circumstance under which an LEA may reduce its local expenditures. If a state establishes a risk pool (i.e., high cost fund) and the state assumes the costs associated with "high cost" children in the LEA, the LEA may reduce its expenditures.[148]

In addition, with some exceptions, an LEA may reduce its local expenditures in certain fiscal years in which its federal allocation exceeds the amount received in the previous fiscal year by not more than 50% of the excess amount.[149] These funds must be used to carry out activities authorized under ESEA.[150] Exceptions include the following: (1) the state is required to prohibit an LEA from reducing its MOE if the SEA has taken responsibility for providing FAPE in the LEA because the LEA is unable to establish and maintain programs of FAPE, or the state has taken action against the LEA under IDEA's enforcement provisions;[151] (2) if in its annual determination on the performance of LEAs, a state determines that an LEA does not meet requirements (i.e., the LEA needs assistance, intervention, or substantial intervention), the state must prohibit the LEA from reducing its MOE;[152] and (3) the amount of funds expended by an LEA for CEIS[153]must count toward the maximum amount of the reduction in expenditures the LEA may make.[154] Consequently, any LEA that is required to use 15% of its allocation on CEIS because the state has determined that "significant disproportionality"[155] based on race and ethnicity is occurring would be prohibited from reducing its MOE.[156]

Supplement, Not Supplant

Both states and LEAs must use IDEA funds to supplement state, local, and other federal funds and not to supplant them.[157] As with the state MOE requirement, the Secretary of Education has authority to grant a waiver of the state-level SNS requirement if the state provides "clear and convincing evidence" that all children with disabilities in the state have FAPE available.[158] If an LEA (or state) maintains its level of local, or state and local, expenditures for special education and related services from year to year, then the LEA has met its MOE and SNS requirements. There are no SNS or MOE waiver provisions for LEAs.[159]

Compliance

Monitoring

The Secretary monitors the implementation of IDEA through the oversight of states' required general supervision of the implementation of IDEA requirements, and through the states' required state performance plans (SPP).[160] These plans evaluate a state's efforts to implement the requirements and purposes of IDEA and describe how the state will improve implementation.[161] The Secretary must enforce IDEA[162] and must also require states to monitor and enforce the implementation of IDEA by LEAs.[163] The primary focus of federal and state monitoring is on improving educational results and functional outcomes for all children with disabilities and ensuring that states meet IDEA program requirements.[164] IDEA specifies three priority areas that are to be monitored by the Secretary regarding states, and by states regarding LEAs, using quantifiable indicators to measure performance. These three monitoring priorities are:

- provision of a free appropriate public education in the least restrictive environment;
- state exercise of general supervisory authority, including child find, effective monitoring, the use of resolution sessions, mediation, voluntary binding arbitration, and a system of transition services; and
- disproportionate representation of racial and ethnic groups in special education and related services, to the extent the representation is the result of inappropriate identification.[165]

As part of an SPP,[166] each state must establish measurable and rigorous targets for the indicators established by the Secretary in the three priority areas.[167] Each state must use the targets established in its SPP and the three priority areas to analyze the performance of each LEA in the state.[168] In addition, each state must report annually to the Secretary on the state's performance under the SPP.[169] Annual state reporting of performance on the SPP indicators is done through the Annual Performance Report (APR).[170] The state must report annually to the public on the performance of each LEA.[171] This annual report must be made as soon as practicable, but no later than 120 days following the state's submission of its APR to the Secretary.[172] The state must also make available through public means the state's SPP, APR, and the state's annual report on the performance of each LEA in the state. At a minimum, the state must post these items on the SEA's website and distribute them to the media and through public agencies.[173]

Enforcement

Based on the information provided by the state in the SPP, information from monitoring visits, and any other public information made available, the Secretary shall determine annually if the state

- meets the requirements and purposes of IDEA Part B,
- needs assistance in implementing the requirements of IDEA Part B,
- needs intervention in implementing the requirements of IDEA Part B, or
- needs substantial intervention in implementing the requirements of IDEA Part B.

If the Secretary makes a determination that a state needs intervention or substantial intervention, the Secretary must provide notice and an opportunity for a hearing.[174]

If the Secretary determines that a state does not meet requirements, IDEA specifies a number of enforcement actions depending on the Secretary's specific determination. These actions range from advising the state of available sources of technical assistance, to requiring the state to prepare a corrective action plan, to withholding, in whole or in part, further IDEA funds to the state. Prior to withholding any funds, the Secretary must provide notice and an opportunity for a hearing.[175] Whenever a state receives notice that the Secretary is proposing to take an enforcement action, the state must, at a minimum, post a notice of the pendency of an action on the SEA's website and distribute the notice to the media and through public agencies.[176]

In its analysis of comments and changes in the regulations, ED notes that

> Neither the Act nor these regulations require SEAs to publicly report on enforcement actions taken against LEAs in the State. The decision to report to the public on enforcement actions imposed on an LEA is best left to each State to decide because individual LEA circumstances vary across each State and no one set of requirements is appropriate in every situation ... However, in the interest of transparency and public accountability, the Department encourages States, where appropriate, to report to the public on any enforcement actions taken against LEAs.[177]

The state must make the same four determinations about LEAs that the Secretary makes about the states.[178] In its analysis of comments and changes in the regulations, ED comments that "States should have some discretion in making annual determination on the performance of their LEAs and, therefore, [ED] decline[s] to establish, in regulation, a uniform process for making annual determinations." ED further notes that it has advised states that in making determinations, they must consider (1) LEA performance on SPP compliance indicators,[179] (2) whether data submitted by an LEA are valid and reliable for each indicator, (3) LEA-specific audit findings, and (4) an uncorrected noncompliance from any source. In addition, ED has advised states to consider performance on results indicators, such as an LEA's graduation and dropout rates or the participation rate of students with disabilities in state assessments.[180] However, the consideration of performance indicators in LEA determinations is not required.

The regulations stipulate the specific enforcement mechanisms that a state must use if the LEA does not meet requirements.[181] These mechanisms include a range of actions and are similar to those that the Secretary must use for state enforcement.[182] The regulations also require that when a state identifies LEA noncompliance with IDEA, it must ensure that the noncompliance is corrected as soon as possible, and no later than one year after the state's identification of the noncompliance.[183]

APPENDIX A. STRUCTURE OF IDEA

Part A—General Provisions

Part A includes congressional findings pertinent to the act, the purposes of the act, and definitions. The definitions included in Part A are of critical importance in interpreting the requirements of the act. These definitions include, among others, definitions of child with a disability, specific learning disability, free appropriate public education, core academic subjects, highly qualified, individualized education program, local educational agency, related services, special education, supplementary aids and services, transition services, and excess costs. These terms have been defined throughout the body of this report.

Part B—Assistance for Education of All Children with Disabilities

Part B provides federal funding for the education of children with disabilities and requires, as a condition for the receipt of such funds, the provision of a free appropriate public education (FAPE) to children with disabilities between the ages of three and 21. School districts must identify, locate, and evaluate all children with disabilities, regardless of the severity of their disability, to determine which children are eligible for special education and related services. Each child receiving services has an Individualized Education Program (IEP), created by an IEP team, delineating the specific special education and related services to be provided to meet his or her needs. The statute also contains procedural safeguards, which are provisions to protect the rights of parents and children with disabilities to ensure the provision of FAPE.

Section 619 of IDEA Part B authorizes grants to states for preschool programs serving children with disabilities ages three to five. Since Part B grants to states are used to serve children with disabilities as young as three years of age (as well as school-age children), Section 619 is not so much a separate program as it is supplementary funding for services to this age group. In general, the provisions, requirements, and guarantees under the grants to states program that apply to school-age children with disabilities also apply to children in this age group. As a result, Section 619 is a relatively brief section of the law and deals mostly with the state and substate funding formulas for the grants and state-level activities.

Part C—Infants and Toddlers with Disabilities

The general purpose of Part C is to aid each state in creating and maintaining "a statewide, comprehensive, coordinated, multidisciplinary, interagency system that provides early intervention services for infants and toddlers with disabilities and their families."[184] Services focus on children from birth through age two who are experiencing or have a high probability of experiencing "developmental delay" (as defined by the state) with respect to physical, mental, or other capacities, and on their families.[185] Services are detailed for each child and his or her family in an Individualized Family Service Plan (IFSP). Services are to be provided, to the maximum extent feasible, in "natural environments," including the home, with other infants and toddlers who are not disabled. States are required to identify a state lead agency, which might be the state educational agency (SEA) but could be other state agencies, to coordinate the program.

Part D—National Activities to Improve Education of Children with Disabilities[186]

Part D authorizes competitive grants to improve the education of children with disabilities in three areas: (1) state personnel development (Subpart 1); (2) personnel preparation, technical assistance, model demonstration projects, and dissemination of information (Subpart 2); and (3) support to improve results for children (Subpart 3).

- Under Subpart 1, competitive grants are made to SEAs for state personnel development grants to assist SEAs "in reforming and improving their systems for personnel preparation and professional development in early intervention, educational, and transitions services ..."[187]

- Under Subpart 2, competitive grants are made to entities such as SEAs, local education agencies (LEAs),[188] institutions of higher education (IHEs), and nonprofit organizations for personnel development to help ensure that there are adequate numbers of personnel with skills and knowledge needed to help children with disabilities succeed,[189] for technical assistance and dissemination of material based on knowledge gained through research and practice,[190] and for studies and evaluations.[191]
- Under Subpart 3, competitive grants are made to nonprofit organizations for parent training and information centers, which provide parents of children with disabilities with needed training and information to work with professionals in meeting the early intervention and special education needs of their children.[192] Also, under Subpart 3, competitive grants are made to entities such as SEAs, LEAs, IHEs, and nonprofit organizations for research, development, and other activities that promote the use of technology in providing special education and early intervention services.[193]

APPENDIX B. COMMONLY USED ACRONYMS

APPE	Average Per Pupil Expenditure
APR	Annual Performance Report
CEIS	Coordinated Early Intervening Services
ED	U.S. Department of Education
ESEA	Elementary and Secondary Education Act
FAPE	Free Appropriate Public Education
IDEA	The Individuals with Disabilities Education Act
IEP	Individualized Education Program
LEA	Local Educational Agency
MOE	Maintenance of Effort
RTI	Response to Intervention
SEA	State Education Agency
SNS	Supplement, Not Supplant
SPP	State Performance Plan

End Notes

[1] 20 U.S.C. §1400 et seq.

[2] U.S. Department of Education, National Center for Education Statistics, Institute for Education Sciences, *The Condition of Education 2010* , May 2010, p.34, http://nces.ed.gov/pubs2010 /2010028.pdf.

[3] The name was changed to the Individuals with Disabilities Education Act by P.L. 101-476. The public law also substituted the phrase "children with disabilities" for the phrase "handicapped children" throughout the act.

[4] 20 U.S.C. §1401(b), P.L. 94-142 §601(b).

[5] For more information on each of the factors that contributed to the enactment of P.L. 94-142, see CRS Report 95-669, *The Individuals with Disabilities Education Act: Congressional Intent*, by Nancy Lee Jones.

[6] For a discussion of the 2004 amendments made by P.L. 108-446, see CRS Report RL32716, *Individuals with Disabilities Education Act (IDEA): Analysis of Changes Made by P.L. 108-446*, by Ann Lordeman and Nancy Lee Jones. For an overview of the IDEA regulations from the Department of Education, see CRS Report RL33649, *The Individuals with Disabilities Education Act (IDEA): Final Regulations for P.L. 108-446*, and CRS Report R40055, *The Individuals with Disabilities Education Act: Final Part B Regulations.*

[7] IDEA authorizes appropriations for Part C and Part D programs and activities through FY2010. These authorities were automatically extended for an additional fiscal year by the General Education Provisions Act (GEPA; 20 U.S.C.§1226a). Funding for the programs continues to be authorized through annual appropriations.

[8] 20 U.S.C. §1400(d)(1), P.L. 108-446 §601(d)(1).

[9] 20 U.S.C §14001(3)(A), P.L. 108-446 §602(3)(A), and 34 C.F.R. §300.8. The statute at §602(3)(B) also permits the state and LEA to include as a child with a disability a child age three through nine, or any subset of that range, who is experiencing developmental delays—as defined by the state and as measured by appropriate diagnostic instruments and procedures—in physical, cognitive, communication, social, emotional, or adaptive development. The child must also require special education and related services because of the developmental delay.

[10] 29 U.S.C. §794. For more information on Section 504, see CRS Report RL34041, *Section 504 of the Rehabilitation Act of 1973: Prohibiting Discrimination Against Individuals with Disabilities in Programs or Activities Receiving Federal Assistance*, coordinated by Cynthia Brougher.

[11] 42 U.S.C. §12101 et seq. For a more detailed discussion of the ADA, see CRS Report 98-921, *The Americans with Disabilities Act (ADA): Statutory Language and Recent Issues*, by Cynthia Brougher and James V. DeBergh.

[12] See citation to Rachel A. Holler and Perry A. Zirkel, "Section 504 and Public Schools: A National Survey Concerning 'Section 504-Only' Students," 92 NASSP Bulletin 19, 28 (March 2008) in CRS Report R40123, Education of Individuals with Disabilities: The Individuals with Disabilities Education Act (IDEA), Section 504 of the Rehabilitation Act, and the Americans with Disabilities Act (ADA), by Nancy Lee Jones. For more information on differences among IDEA, Section 504, and the ADA, see this report.

[13] A specific learning disability is defined as "a disorder in 1 or more of the basic psychological processes involved in understanding or in using language, spoken or written, which may manifest itself in the imperfect ability to listen, think, speak, read, write, spell, or do mathematical calculations." 20 U.S.C. §1401(30)(A), P.L. 108-446 §601(30)(A).

[14] 20 U.S.C. §1401(30)(B), P.L. 108-446 §601(30)(B). Specific learning disabilities do not include learning problems that are primarily the result of visual, hearing, or motor disabilities; of mental retardation; of emotional disturbance; or of environmental, cultural, or economic disadvantage. 20 U.S.C §1401(30)(C), P.L. 108-446 §601(30)(C).

[15] The regulations at 34 C.F.R. §300.102 (2010) specify three exceptions to this requirement: (1) children ages 3, 4, 5, 18, 19, 20, or 21 in a state that does not provide a public education to children of those ages, (2) children ages 18 through 21 incarcerated in an adult correctional facility who were not identified as children with disabilities in their last educational placement; and (3) children with disabilities who have graduated from high school with a regular high school diploma.

[16] 20 U.S.C. §1401(9), P.L. 108-446 §601(9). For information on the legal aspects of FAPE, see CRS Report RL33444, *The Individuals with Disabilities Education Act (IDEA): Supreme Court Decisions*, by Nancy Lee Jones and Carol J. Toland; CRS Report R40521, *The Individuals with Disabilities Education Act (IDEA): Selected Judicial Developments Following the 2004 Reauthorization*, by Nancy Lee Jones; and CRS Report R40690, *The Individuals with Disabilities Education Act (IDEA): Statutory Provisions and Recent Legal Issues*, coordinated by Cynthia Brougher.

[17] 34 C.F.R. §300.101(a) (2010).

[18] 34 C.F.R. §300.101(c) (2010).

[19] 20 U.S.C §1412(a)(3), P.L. 108-446 §612(a)(3).

[20] 20 U.S.C. §1414(a), P.L. 108-446 §414(a). This subsection contains the requirements for evaluations, parental consent, and reevaluations.

[21] The LEA may refuse the parent's request for an initial evaluation if it does not suspect that the child has a disability. However, the public agency must provide written notice to the parents, consistent with 34 C.F.R. §300.503(b)(2010) and §615(c)(1) of the act, which explains, among other things, why the public agency refuses to conduct an initial evaluation and the information that was used as the basis to make that decision. The parent may challenge such a refusal by requesting a due process hearing. (71 Fed. Reg. 46636 (August 14, 2006)).

[22] The term "consent" is defined at 34 C.F.R. §300.9, and means, in part, that "the parent has been fully informed of all information relevant to the activity for which consent is sought, in his or her native language, or other mode of communication"; For more information on parental consent, see also 34 C.F.R. §300.300 (2010).

[23] In addition, at the time of the referral or parent request for evaluation, the LEA must provide the parent with the "Procedural Safeguards Notice," which is a comprehensive written explanation of IDEA's legal rights and protections for children with disabilities and their parents. See 20 U.S.C. §1415(d), P.L. 108-446 §615(d). For further information on procedural safeguards, see "Procedural Safeguards " in this report.

[24] 20 U.S.C §1414(a)(1), P.L. 108-446 §614 (a)(1).

[25] 20 U.S.C. §1414(b)(2), P.L. 108-446 §614 (b)(2).

[26] For all the provisions related to additional requirements, see 20 U.S.C. §1414(b)(3), P.L. 108-446 §614 (b)(3).

[27] 20 U.S.C. §1414(b)(4)(A), P.L. 108-446 §614 (b)(4)(A).

[28] 20 U.S.C §1414(b)(4)(B), P.L. 108-446 §614 (b)(4)(B).

[29] 20 U.S.C. §1414(b)(5), P.L. 108-446 §614 (b)(5).

[30] 20 U.S.C. §1414(a)(2), P.L. 108-446 §614 (a)(2).

[31] 34 C.F.R. §300.300(c) (2010).

[32] 20 U.S.C. §1414(c)(5), P.L. 108-446 §614 (c)(5).

[33] 20 U.S.C. §1414(b)(6), P.L. 108-446 §614 (b)(6), and 34 C.F.R. §300.307 through §300.311 (2010).

[34] 34 C.F.R. §300.307 (2010).

[35] 20 U.S.C. §1414(b)(6)(A), P.L. 108-446 §614 (b)(6)(A), and 34 C.F.R. §300.307(a)(1) (2010). The Senate report in considering the 2004 amendments to IDEA explains the rationale for this provision:

The committee believes that the IQ-achievement discrepancy formula, which considers whether a child has a severe discrepancy between achievement and intellectual ability, should not be a requirement for determining eligibility under the IDEA. There is no evidence that the IQ-achievement discrepancy formula can be applied in a consistent and educationally meaningful (i.e., reliable and valid) manner. In addition, this approach has been found to be particularly problematic for students living in poverty or culturally and linguistically different backgrounds, who may be erroneously viewed as having intrinsic intellectual limitations when their difficulties on such tests really reflect lack of experience or educational opportunity. S.Rept. 108-185, 108th Cong., 2d Sess. 26 (2003).

[36] 20 U.S.C. §1414(b)(6)(B), P.L. 108-446 §614 (b)(6)(B).

[37] 34 C.F.R. §300.307(a)(3)(2010). In ED's analysis of comments and changes to the final regulations at 71 Fed. Reg. 46648 (August 14, 2006), ED elaborates on this criterion by stating: "For example, a state could choose to identify children based on absolute low achievement and consideration of exclusionary factors as one criterion for eligibility. Other alternatives might combine features of different models for identification."

[38] 34 C.F.R. §300.308 (2010).

[39] 34 C.F.R. §300.309(a) (2010).

[40] These eight areas are oral expression, listening comprehension, written expression, basic reading skill, reading fluency skills, reading comprehension, mathematics calculation, and mathematics problem solving.

[41] 34 C.F.R. §300.309(b) (2010).

[42] 34 C.F.R. §300.309 (c). In ED's analysis of comments and changes to the final regulations at 71 Fed. Reg. 46658 (August 14, 2006), ED addresses the issue of "an appropriate period of time" by stating "Instructional models vary in terms of the length of time required for the intervention to have the intended effect on a child's progress. It would not be appropriate for the Department to establish timelines ... because doing so would make it difficult for LEAs to implement models specific to their local school districts. These decisions are best left to state and local professionals who have knowledge of the instructional methods used in their school."

[43] 34 C.F.R. §300.310 (2010).

[44] 34 C.F.R. §300.311 (2010).

[45] 20 U.S.C §1414(d)(3)(A), P.L. 108-446 §614 (d)(3)(A).

[46] 20 U.S.C. §1414(d)(4), P.L. 108-446 §614 (d)(4).

[47] 34 C.F.R. §300.323(c) (2010).

[48] 20 U.S.C. §1414(d)(1)(A), P.L. 108-446 §614 (d)(1)(A).

[49] An accommodation is a change in instructional material or assessment practices that enable students with disabilities to reduce barriers to learning.

[50] Although many students with disabilities are able to participate in the general state assessment, other students may need an alternate assessment that is tailored to their needs and allows them to more accurately demonstrate what they know and can do. For information on alternate assessments for students with disabilities, see CRS Report R40701, *Alternate Assessments for Students with Disabilities*, by Erin D. Lomax.

[51] As defined at 20 U.S.C. §1401(34), P.L. 108-446 §602(34), transition services mean a coordinated set of activities for a child with a disability that—(A) is designed to be within a results-oriented process, that is focused on improving the academic and functional achievement of the child with a disability to facilitate the child's movement from school to post-school activities, including post-secondary education, vocational education, integrated employment (including supported employment), continuing and adult education, adult services, independent living, or community participation; (B) is based on the individual child's needs, taking into account the child's strengths, preferences, and interests; and (C) includes instruction, related services, community experiences, the development of employment and other post-school adult living objectives, and, when appropriate, acquisition of daily living skills and functional vocational evaluation.

[52] 20 U.S.C. §1414(d)(1)(B), P.L. 108-446 §614 (d)(1)(B).

[53] If the purpose of an IEP meeting is to consider the postsecondary goals for the child and transition services, the LEA must invite the child to attend the meeting; 34 C.F.R. §300.321(b)(1) (2010).

[54] 20 U.S.C. §1401(29), P.L. 108-446 §602(29), and 34 C.F.R. §300.39 (2010).

[55] 34 C.F.R. §300.39(b)(1) (2010).

[56] 20 U.S.C. §1401(26), P.L. 108-446 §602(26), and 34 C.F.R. §300.34 (2010).

[57] For a discussion of the legal issues regarding medical services as a related service, see CRS Report R40690, *The Individuals with Disabilities Education Act (IDEA): Statutory Provisions and Recent Legal Issues*, coordinated by Cynthia Brougher.

[58] An LEA cannot use the full 15% for CEIS when they are also reducing funds under IDEA maintenance of effort (MOE) provisions. See the discussion in this report on "Maintenance of Effort (MOE)" for further explanation.

[59] 20 U.S.C. §1413(f), P.L. 107-110 §613(f). Coordinated Early Intervening Services (CEIS), also referred to in statute as Early Intervening Serving (EIS), should not be confused with Early *Intervention* Services (EIS) authorized under Part C of IDEA. Part C, EIS, defined in Section 632(4), is for infants and toddlers with disabilities, while Part B CEIS is for students who are not currently identified as having disabilities but need additional support to succeed in a general education environment. (A student could receive CEIS if he or she had previously received special education, but is not currently identified as needing it. 71 Fed. Reg. 46626 (August 14, 2006) and 34 C.F.R. §300.226 (2010).)

[60] 34 C.F.R. §300.226 (c) (2010).

[61] 71 Fed. Reg. 46626-46627 (August 14, 2006).

[62] For more information on CEIS, see U.S. Department of Education, "Memorandum: Coordinated Early Intervening Services (CEIS) Under Part B of the Individuals with Disabilities Education Act (IDEA)," July 28, 2008, http://www2.ed.gov/policy

[63] 20 U.S.C §1413(f)(5), P.L. 107-110 §613(f)(5).

[64] The term "significant disproportionality" is defined by each state; 71.Fed. Reg. 46738 (August 14, 2006).

[65] 20 U.S.C. §1418(d), P.L. 108-446 §618(d).

[66] 34 C.F.R. §300.646 (b)(2) (2010).

[67] U.S. Department of Education, *Implementing RTI Using Title I, Title III, and CEIS Funds, Key Issues for Decision-maker*, p. 11, http://www2.ed.gov/programs/titleiparta /rtifiles /rti.pdf.

[68] U.S. Department of Education, *Questions and Answers on Response to Intervention (RTI) and Early Intervening Services (EIS)*, January 2007, Question F-5. RTI is one type of scientific, research-based intervention used to identify students with SLD. See "Identifying and Evaluating a Child with a Specific Learning Disability (SLD)."

[69] 20 U.S.C. §1412(a)(14)(C), P.L. 108-446 §612(a)(14)(C).

[70] The term "core academic subjects" as defined in ESEA at 20 U.S.C. §7801(11), P.L. 107-110 §9101(11) means "English, reading or language arts, mathematics, science, foreign languages, civics and government, economics, arts, history, and geography." The IDEA definition of core academic subjects defined at 20 U.S.C. §1401(4), P.L. 108-446 §602(4) has the same meaning as the ESEA definition.

[71] 20 U.S.C. §7801(23), P.L. 107-110 §9101(23). For more information on ESEA requirements, see CRS Report RL33333, *A Highly Qualified Teacher in Every Classroom: Implementation of the No Child Left Behind Act and Reauthorization Issues for the 112th Congress*, by Jeffrey J. Kuenzi (available from the author).

[72] For more information on highly qualified teachers under IDEA, see CRS Report RL33649, *The Individuals with Disabilities Education Act (IDEA): Final Regulations for P.L. 108-446*, by Nancy Lee Jones and Ann Lordeman.

[73] 20 U.S.C. §1401(10), P.L. 108-446 §602(10), and 34 C.F.R. §300.18.

[74] 20 U.S.C. §1412(a)(5), P.L. 108-446 §612(a)(5). For legal issues pertaining to least restrictive environment, see CRS Report R40690, *The Individuals with Disabilities Education Act (IDEA): Statutory Provisions and Recent Legal Issues*, coordinated by Cynthia Brougher.

[75] 20 U.S.C. §1401(33), P.L. 108-446 §602(33). Supplementary aids and services are defined as "aids, services, and other supports that are provided in regular education classes or other education-related settings to enable children with disabilities to be educated with nondisabled children to the maximum extent appropriate in accordance with section 612(a)(5) [Least Restrictive Environment]."

[76] 34 C.F.R. §300.115.

[77] 34 C.F.R. §300.116.

[78] 34 C.F.R. §300.503.

[79] For more information on this topic, including legal issues, see CRS Report R41678, The Individuals with Disabilities Education Act (IDEA): Private Schools, by Nancy Lee Jones.

[80] 20 U.S.C. §1412(a)(10)(B), P.L. 108-446 §612(a)(10)(B).

[81] 20 U.S.C. §1412(a)(10)(B), P.L. 108-446 §612(a)(10)(B).

[82] 20 U.S.C. §1412(a)(10)(C), P.L. 108-446 §612(a)(10)(C). Specifically, an LEA could be required by a court or a hearing officer to reimburse the parents of a child with a disability who (1) previously received special education and related services from an LEA, and (2) enrolled the child in a private elementary school or secondary school without the consent of or referral by the LEA for the cost of the private school enrollment if the court or hearing officer found that the LEA had not made FAPE available to the child in a timely manner prior to the private school enrollment.

[83] 20 U.S.C. §1412(a)(10)(iii)(I), P.L. 108-446 §612(a)(10)(iii)(I). For example, if an LEA has 250 children with disabilities, 15 of whom were parentally placed in a private school, 6% of federal IDEA Part B funds (i.e., 15/250 * 100) would be spent on the group of children with disabilities in private schools in the LEA. For a more comprehensive hypothetical example, see Appendix B to 34 C.F.R. Part 300. It should be emphasized that no individual parentally placed private school child with a disability is entitled to services.

[84] 20 U.S.C. §1412(a)(10)(A)(iii), P.L. 108-446 §612(a)(10)(A)(iii).

[85] 34 C.F.R. §300.137(b) (2010).

[86] 34 C.F.R. §300.138)(b) (2010).

[87] For information on the legal issues pertaining to procedural safeguards, including burden of proof, parental rights, attorneys' and expert witness fees, see CRS Report R40690, *The*

Individuals with Disabilities Education Act (IDEA): Statutory Provisions and Recent Legal Issues, coordinated by Cynthia Brougher.

[88] 20 U.S.C. §1415(b)(1), P.L. 108-446 §615(b)(1), and 34 C.F.R. §300.501(a) (2010).

[89] 20 U.S.C. §1414(e), P.L. 108-446 §614(e), and 34 C.F.R. §300.501(b) and (c) (2010).

[90] 20 U.S.C. §1415(b)(1), P.L. 108-446 §614(b)(1), and 34 C.F.R. §300.502 (2010). If the LEA asserts that its evaluation is appropriate, it can file a due process complaint to request a hearing. If the final decision is that the agency's evaluation is appropriate, the parent still has the right to an independent education evaluation, but not at public expense.

[91] 20 U.S.C. §1415 (b)(3) and (4), P.L. 108-446 §615(b)(3) and (4), and 34 C.F.R. §300.503(a) and (c) (2010). For the statutory and regulatory provision regarding the content of the notice, see 20 U.S.C. §1415 (c)(1), P.L. 108-446 §615(c)(1), and 34 C.F.R. §300.503(b) (2010).

[92] 20 U.S.C. §1415(d), P.L. 108-446 §615(d), and 34 C.F.R. §300.504 (2010).

[93] 20 U.S.C. §1415(e), P.L. 108-446 §615(e), and 34 C.F.R. §300.506 (2010).

[94] 20 U.S.C. §1415(f) through (j), P.L. 108-446 §615(f) through (j), and 34 C.F.R. §300.507 through §300.518 (2010).

[95] 34 C.F.R. §300.151 through §300.153 (2010). State complaint procedures are not contained in the statute.

[96] 20 U.S.C. §1415(e), P.L. 108-446 §615(e), and 34 C.F.R. §300.506 (2010).

[97] 20 U.S.C. §1415(j), P.L. 108-446 §615(j), and 34 C.F.R. §300.518 (2010).

[98] 20 U.S.C. §1415(b)(7) and (8), and 20 U.S.C. §1415(c)(2), P.L. 108-446 §615(b)(7) and (8), and §615(c)(2), and 34 C.F.R. §300.507 through §300.509 (2010).

[99] There are two exceptions to this timeline. The timeline does not apply if the parent was prevented from requesting a hearing due to specific misrepresentations by the LEA that it had resolved the problem forming the basis of the due process complaint; or the LEA withheld information from the parent that was required to be provided to the parent. 20 U.S.C. §1415(b)(6), P.L. 108-446 §615(b)(6), and 34 C.F.R. §300.507(a)(2) (2010).

[100] For more detail, see the statutory and regulatory provisions at 20 U.S.C. §1415, P.L. 108-446 §615, and 34 C.F.R. Subpart E (2010).

[101] For information on conducting a due process hearing, see 20 U.S.C. §1415(f), P.L. 108-446 §615(f), and 34 C.F.R. §300.511 through §300.515 (2010). For information on the required qualifications of the hearing officer, see 20 U.S.C. §1415(f)(3), P.L. 108-446 §615(f)(3), and 34 C.F.R. §300.511(c) (2010).

[102] 20 U.S.C. §1415(g) and (i), P.L. 108-446 §615(g) and (i), and 34 C.F.R. §300.514 and §300.516 (2010).

[103] 34 C.F.R. §300.151 through §300.153 (2010).

[104] 71 Fed. Reg. 46700 (August 14, 2006).

[105] An extension of the 60-day time limit may be permitted only if exceptional circumstances exist with respect to a particular complaint or if the complainant and the LEA agree to extend the time to engage in mediation, or to engage in other alternative means of dispute resolution, if available in the state.

[106] For more information on IDEA disciplinary provisions, see CRS Report RL32753, *Individuals with Disabilities Education Act (IDEA): Discipline Provisions in P.L. 108-446*, by Nancy Lee Jones. For information on legal issues, see discussion of Honig v. Doe in CRS Report RL33444, *The Individuals with Disabilities Education Act (IDEA): Supreme Court Decisions*, by Nancy Lee Jones and Carol J. Toland.

[107] U.S. Department of Education, *Questions and Answers on Discipline Procedures*, June 2009, http://idea.ed.gov/ explore/view/p/%2Croot%2Cdynamic%2CQaCorner%2C7%2C.

[108] 20 U.S.C. §1415(k).

[109] 20 U.S.C. §1415(k)(1)(B), P.L. 108-446 §615(k)(1)(B).

[110] 20 U.S.C. §1415(k)(1)(G), P.L. 108-446 §615(k)(1)(G).

[111] 20 U.S.C. §1415(k)(3), P.L. 108-446 §615(k)(3).

[112] To determine if the child's behavior meets either of these criteria, the LEA, the parent, and the relevant members of the IEP team must review all relevant information in the student's file, including the child's IEP, any teacher observations, and any relevant information provided by the parents; 20 U.S.C. §1415(k)(1)(E), P.L. 108-446 §615(k)(1)(E).

[113] 71 Fed. Reg. 46720 (August 14, 2006).

[114] 20 U.S.C. §1415(k)(1)(C), P.L. 108-446 §615(k)(1)(C).

[115] 20 U.S.C. §1415(k)(1)(F)(i), P.L. 108-446 §615(k)(1)(F)(i). In addition, if the conduct of a child with a disability was the direct result of the LEA's failure to implement the IEP, "the LEA must take immediate steps to remedy those deficiencies"; 34 C.F.R. §300.530(e)(3) (2010).

[116] 20 U.S.C. §1415(k)(1)(F)(ii), P.L. 108-446 §615(k)(1)(F)(ii).

[117] 20 U.S.C. §1415(k)(1)(F)(iii), P.L. 108-446 §615(k)(1)(F)(iii).

[118] 20 U.S.C. §1415(k)(3)(A), P.L. 108-446 §615(k)(3)(A).

[119] 20 U.SC. §1415(k)(6), P.L. 108-446 §615(k)(6).

[120] The term "excess costs" is defined at 20 U.S.C. §1401 (8), P.L. 108-446 §602(8).

[121] "In 1975, when the act was originally enacted, Congress established the goal of providing up to 40% of the national average per pupil expenditure to assist states and local educational agencies with the excess costs of educating students with disabilities"; H.Rept. 108-77, p.93.

[122] CRS calculation based on unpublished data from the U.S. Department of Education.

[123] 20 U.S.C. §1411(b)(1), P.L. 108-446 §616(b)(1). The outlying areas are defined in §602(22) as the "United States Virgin Islands, Guam, American Samoa, and the Commonwealth of the Northern Mariana Islands." Freely associated states are defined in §611(b)(3) as "the Republic of the Marshall Islands, the Federated States of Micronesia, and the Republic of Palau."

[124] The statute at §611(b)(2) reserves 1.226% of the Part B appropriation for the Department of the Interior's Bureau of Indian Education (BIE) schools; however, this percentage has been overridden since FY2002 through the appropriations process, which has provided annual increases for BIE schools based on the rate of inflation. For example, see the language in the Special Education account in Title III of Division D of P.L. 111-117 (Consolidated Appropriations Act, 2010).

[125] 20 U.S.C. §1411(c), P.L. 108-446 §616(c).

[126] 20 U.S.C. §1411(d), P.L. 108-446 §616(d).

[127] These age ranges for this population vary from state to state depending on the age range for which each state makes FAPE available.

[128] 20 U.S.C. §1411(d)(3)(B) and 20 U.S.C. §1411(a)(2)(B), P.L. 108-446 §616(d)(3)(B) and P.L. 108-446 §616(a)(2)(B).

[129] 20 U.S.C. §1411(d)(4), P.L. 108-446 §611(d)(4).

[130] 20 U.S.C. §1411(e)(1), P.L. 108-446 §611(e)(1). The amount that a state may reserve for administration is up to the greater of the maximum amount the state could reserve from FY2004 funds, or $800,000, increased by the Secretary for inflation as reflected by the Consumer Price Index for All Urban Consumers.

[131] 20 U.S.C. §1411(e)(2)(B), P.L. 108-446 §611(e)(2)(B).

[132] 20 U.S.C. §1411(e)(2)(C), P.L. 108-446 §611(e)(2)(C).

[133] 20 U.S.C. §1411(e)(3), P.L. 108-446 §611(e)(3). The percentage of a state's allocation that a state may reserve for state-level activities depends on the amount a state uses for state administration and whether or not the state uses a risk pool. A state that uses a risk pool can set aside 10.5% for state level activities if it uses $850,000 or less for state administration, or 10% if it uses $850,000 or more for state administration A state that does *not* use a risk pool can set aside 9.5% for state level activities if it uses $850,000 or less for state administration, or 9% if it uses $850,000 or more for state administration. For FY2007 and each subsequent fiscal year, each state may reserve the maximum amount the state was eligible to reserve in FY2006, cumulatively adjusted by the rate of inflations as reflected by the Consumer Price Index for All Urban Consumers. See 20 U.S.C. §1411(e)(2)(A), P.L. 108-446 §611(e)(2)(A).

[134] 20 U.S.C. §1411(e)(3)(C), P.L. 108-446 §611(e)(3)(C).

[135] 20 U.S.C. §1411(e)(3)(D)(iii), P.L. 108-446 §611(e)(3)(D)(iii).

[136] 20 U.S.C. §1411(e)(3)(E), P.L. 108-446 §611(e)(3)(E).

[137] 20 U.S.C. §1411(e)(3)(I), P.L. 108-446 §611(e)(3)(I).

[138] 20 U.S.C. §1411(f), P.L. 108-446 §611(f).

[139] 20 U.S.C. §1412(a)(18)(A), P.L. 108-446 §612(a)(18)(A).

[140] 20 U.S.C. §1412(a)(18)(B), P.L. 108-446 §612(a)(18)(B).

[141] 20 U.S.C. §1412(a)(18)(C)(i), P.L. 108-446 §612(a)(18)(C)(i).

[142] 20 U.S.C. §1412(a)(18)(C)(ii), P.L. 108-446 §612(a)(18)(C)(ii).

[143] 20 U.S.C. §1412(a)(18)(D), P.L. 108-446 §612(a)(18)(D).

[144] For information on how an LEA calculates its excess costs, see Appendix A to Part 300, 34 C.F.R.

[145] 20 U.S.C. §1413(a)(2)(A), P.L. 108-446 §613(a)(2)(A).

[146] 34 C.F.R. §300.203(b) (2010). In practice, the MOE requirement is based on a comparison of non-federal expenditures for special education services for pupils with disabilities in the preceding fiscal year to those for the second preceding fiscal year since that would be the most recently available data.

[147] 20 U.S.C. §1413(a)(2)(B), P.L. 108-446 §613(a)(2)(B).

[148] 34 C.F.R. §300.204(e) (2010). See, also, the discussion in the report on "State-Level Activities."

[149] 20 U.S.C. §1413(a)(2)(C)(i), P.L. 108-446 §613(a)(2)(C)(i).

[150] 20 U.S.C. §1413(a)(2)(C)(ii), P.L. 108-446 §613(a)(2)(C)(ii).

[151] 20 U.S.C. §1413(a)(2)(C)(iii), P.L. 108-446 §613(a)(2)(C)(iii).

[152] 20 U.S.C. §1416(f), P.L. 108-446 §616(f). See the section in this report on "Enforcement" for more information on the federal and state performance determinations. Also, see U.S. Department of Education, *Modifications to Questions in the April 2009 Guidance on the Individuals with Disabilities Education Act, Part B, April 13, 2009*, D-7.

[153] For information on CEIS, see the section of this report on "Coordinated Early Intervening Services (CEIS)".

[154] 20 U.S.C. §1413(a)(2)(C)(iv), P.L. 108-446 §613(a)(2)(C)(iv).

[155] For information on "significant disproportionality," see the section of this report on "Coordinated Early Intervening Services (CEIS)."

[156] U.S. Department of Education, *Modifications to Questions in the April 2009 Guidance on the Individuals with Disabilities Education Act, Part B, April 13, 1009*, D-7. The amount of funds an LEA uses for CEIS for reducing the MOE in years when there is an increase in the LEA allocation is interrelated. The decision about one use will affect the amount of funds

available for the other use. For information on the interaction of CEIS and MOE, see Appendix D to Part 300, 34 C.F.R.

[157] 20 U.S.C. §1412(a)172)(C), P.L. 108-446 §613(a)(17)(C).

[158] Ibid. See 34 C.F.R. §300.164 for standards for applying for this waiver.

[159] U.S. Department of Education, *Guidance: Funds for Part B of the Individuals with Disabilities Education Act made Available Under the American Recovery and Reinvestment Act of 2009*, April 2009, C-6.

[160] 20 U.S.C. §1416(a)(1)(A), P.L. 108-446 §616(a)(1)(A).

[161] 20 U.S.C. §1416(b)(1)(A), P.L. 108-446 §616(b)(1)(A).

[162] 20 U.S.C. §1416(a)(1)(B), P.L. 108-446 §616(a)(1)(B).

[163] 20 U.S.C. § 1416(a)(1)(C), P.L. 108-446 §616(a)(1)(C).

[164] 20 U.S.C. §1416(a)(2), P.L. 108-446 §616(a)(2).

[165] 20 U.S.C. §1416(a)(3), P.L. 108-446 §616(a)(3). Each state must have in effect policies and procedures designed to prevent the inappropriate over-identification or disproportionate representation by race and ethnicity of children as children with disabilities (20 U.S.C. §1412(a)(24), P.L. 108-446 §612(a)(24)).

[166] Each state must review its SPP at least once every six years and amendments must be submitted to the Secretary; 20 U.S.C. §1416(b(1)(C), P.L. 108-446 §616(b)(1)(C).

[167] 34 C.F.R. §300.601(a)(3) (2010).

[168] 20 U.S.C. §1416(b)(2)(C)(i), P.L. 108-446 §616(b)(2)(C)(i).

[169] 20 U.S.C. §1416(b)(2)(C)(ii)(II), P.L. 108-446 §616(b)(2)(C)(ii)(II).

[170] 20 U.S.C. §1453(d), P.L. 108-446 §653(d).

[171] 20 U.S.C. §1416(b)(2)(C)(ii)(I), P.L. 108-446 §616(b)(2)(C)(ii)(I).

[172] 34 C.F.R. §300.602(b)(i)(A) (2010).

[173] 34 C.F.R. §300.602(b)(i)(B) (2010).

[174] 20 U.S.C. §1416(d), P.L. 108-446 §616(d).

[175] 20 U.S.C. §1416(e), P.L. 108-446 §616(e).

[176] 34 C.F.R. §300.606 (2010). The Secretary also posts the annual determination letters typically issued in June of each year to each state, Puerto Rico, the District of Columbia, and outlying areas on its website at http://www2.ed.gov/fund/ data/report/idea/partbspap/allyears.html.

[177] 71 Fed. Reg. 73203 (August 14, 2006).

[178] 20 U.S.C. §1416(a)(1)(C), P.L. 108-446 §616(a)(1)(C)(ii), and 34 C.F.R. §300.600(a)(2) (2010).

[179] Compliance indicators include, among others, the percent of districts with disproportionate representation of racial and ethnic groups in special education and related services that is the result of inappropriate identification, the percent of children with parental consent to evaluate who were evaluated and had eligibility determined within 60 days (or a state established timeframe), and a general supervision system (including monitoring, complaints, hearings, etc.) that identifies and corrects noncompliance as soon as possible but no later than one year from identification.

[180] 73 Fed. Reg. 73021 (August 14, 2006).

[181] 34 C.F.R. §300.600(a)(3), and 34 C.F.R. §300.800 (2010).

[182] Neither the statute nor the regulations require that states permit LEAs to appeal a state decision. According to ED's guidance *Questions and Answers on Monitoring, Technical Assistance, and Enforcement*, C-11, "Whether a State's determination about an LEA's performance may be appealed is a State decision."

[183] 34 C.F.R. §300.600(e) (2010).

[184] 20 U.S.C. §1431(b)(1), P.L. 108-446 §631(b)(1).

[185] Under certain circumstances, children with disabilities age three and over may continue to receive Part C early intervention services until they are eligible to enter kindergarten; 20 U.S.C. §14345(c), P.L. 108-446 §635(c).

[186] In addition to the statutory provisions in Part D, see the following for more information on these activities: U.S. Department of Education, F*iscal Year 2012, Budget Summary*, pp. 34-36; and U.S. Department of Education, *Guide to U.S. Department of Education Programs,2010*, pp. 254-262.

[187] 20 U.S.C. §1451(a), P.L. 108-446 §651(a).

[188] The term "local educational agency" means "a public board of education or other public authority legally constituted within a State for either administrative control or direction of, or to perform a service function for, public elementary schools or secondary schools in a city, county, township, school district, or other political subdivision of a State, or for such combination of school districts or counties as are recognized in a State as an administrative agency for its public elementary schools or secondary schools." 20 U.S.C. §14011(19), P.L. 108-446 §601(19). The term "school district" is often used instead of local educational agency.

[189] 20 U.S.C. §1462, P.L. 108-446 §662.

[190] 20 U.S.C. §1463, P.L. 108-446 §663.

[191] 20 U.S.C. §1464, P.L. 108-446 §664

[192] 20 U.S.C. §1471, §1472, and §1473, P.L. 108-446 §671, § 672, and §673.

[193] 20 U.S.C. §1474, P.L. 108-446 §674.

In: Individuals with Disabilities Education Act ISBN: 978-1-62808-180-0
Editor: Harold Sanders

Chapter 3

QUESTIONS AND ANSWERS ON RESPONSE TO INTERVENTION (RTI) AND EARLY INTERVENING SERVICES (EIS)*

U.S. Department of Education

The final regulations for the reauthorized Individuals with Disabilities Education Act (IDEA) were published in the Federal Register on August 14, 2006, and became effective on October 13, 2006. Since publication of the final regulations, the Office of Special Education and Rehabilitative Services (OSERS) in the U.S. Department of Education has received requests for clarification of some of these regulations. This is one in a series of question and answer documents prepared by OSERS to address some of the most important issues raised by requests for clarification on a variety of high-interest topics. Generally, the questions, and corresponding answers, presented in this Q&A document required interpretation of IDEA and the regulations and the answers are not simply a restatement of the statutory or regulatory requirements. The responses presented in this document generally are informal guidance representing the interpretation of the Department of the applicable statutory or regulatory requirements in the context of the specific facts presented and are not legally binding. The Q&As are not intended to be a replacement for careful study of IDEA and the regulations. The statute,

* This is an edited, reformatted and augmented version of U.S. Department of Education, dated January 2007.

regulations, and other important documents related to IDEA and the regulations are found at http://idea.ed.gov.

The final regulations incorporate new requirements regarding identifying children with specific learning disabilities (SLD) and early intervening services (EIS). With regard to identifying children with SLD, the regulations: (1) allow a local educational agency (LEA) to consider a child's response to scientific, research-based intervention as part of the SLD determination process; (2) allow States to use other alternative research-based procedures for determining whether a child has a SLD; (3) provide that States may not require the use of a severe discrepancy between intellectual ability and achievement to determine whether a child has a SLD; and (4) require a public agency to use the State criteria in determining whether a child has a SLD and discuss the role that response to scientific research-based interventions plays in a comprehensive evaluation process.

The regulations regarding EIS permit an LEA to use not more than 15% of its IDEA Part B funds to develop and implement EIS. The regulations also indicate how EIS funds can be expended; on whom the EIS funds can be spent; the reporting requirements for EIS; special provisions regarding disproportionality based on race and ethnicity and how that affects an LEA's use of EIS funds; and the relationship of EIS to maintenance of effort. The purpose of the questions and answers that follow is to provide additional guidance to States and LEAs in complying with the requirements regarding EIS and response to scientific research-based interventions to identify students with a SLD.

Authority: The requirements for using a process based on a child's response to scientific, research-based intervention when determining that the child is a child with a specific learning disability are found in the regulations at 34 CFR §§300.307, 300.309 and 300.311.

The requirements for early intervening services are found in the regulations at 34 CFR §§300.205(d), 300.208(a)(2), 300.226 and 300.646(b)(2).

A. General Education vs. Special Education

Question A-1: Please clarify how a child with a disability who is already receiving special education and related services also would be eligible to receive services using response to intervention (RTI) strategies.

Answer: Response to intervention (RTI) strategies are tools that enable educators to target instructional interventions to children's areas of specific need as soon as those needs become apparent. There is nothing in IDEA that prohibits children with disabilities who are receiving special education and related services under IDEA from receiving instruction using RTI strategies unless the use of such strategies is inconsistent with their individualized education programs (IEPs). Additionally, under IDEA, a public agency may use data gathered through RTI strategies in its evaluations and reevaluations of children with SLD. However, children with disabilities who are currently identified as needing special education and related services may not receive RTI services that are funded with IDEA funds used for EIS pursuant to 34 CFR §300.226. This is because EIS is "... for students in kindergarten through grade 12 (with a particular emphasis on students in kindergarten through grade three) who are not currently identified as needing special education or related services, but who need additional academic and behavioral support to succeed in a general education environment."

Question A-2: Why was RTI included in IDEA?

Answer: The reports of both the House and Senate Committees accompanying the IDEA reauthorization bills reflect the Committees' concerns with models of identification of SLD that use IQ tests, and their recognition that a growing body of scientific research supports methods, such as RTI, that more accurately distinguish between children who truly have SLD from those whose learning difficulties could be resolved with more specific, scientifically based, general education interventions. Similarly, the President's Commission on Excellence in Special Education recommended that the identification process for SLD incorporate an RTI approach.

B. Funding

Question B-1: Is the use of funds for EIS required or permitted?

Answer: Generally, the use of funds an LEA receives under Part B of the Act for EIS is discretionary on the part of the LEA, except when an LEA has significant disproportionality based on race and ethnicity. Under 34 CFR §300.226, an LEA may not use more than 15% of the amount the LEA receives under Part B of the Act for any fiscal year, less any amount reduced by the LEA pursuant to 34 CFR §300.205, if any, in combination with other amounts (which may include amounts other than education funds), to develop and implement coordinated EIS. If a State identifies an LEA as having significant disproportionality based on race and ethnicity with respect to the identification of children with disabilities, the placement of children with disabilities in particular educational settings, or the incidence, duration, and type of disciplinary actions taken against children with disabilities, including suspensions and expulsions, the SEA must require the LEA to reserve the maximum amount of funds available to the LEA to provide EIS to children in the LEA, particularly, but not exclusively, to children in those groups that were significantly overidentified.

Question B-2: What does it mean to "reserve" funds for EIS?

Answer: The Department interprets "reserve" to mean that these funds can only be spent on EIS. The statute does not authorize LEAs to use the funds they must "reserve" for EIS for any other purpose.

Question B-3: Must the maximum amount of special education funds allowed for EIS be reserved only if significant disproportionality is the result of inappropriate identification?

Answer: No. The reservation of funds must occur whether or not the significant disproportionality was the result of inappropriate identification. In addition to identification, funds also would have to be reserved if significant disproportionality was found with respect to discipline or placement in particular educational settings.

Question B-4: If a State has identified significant disproportionality in an LEA can the IDEA funds the LEA must use to address the issue be used to provide services to students who have already been found eligible for special education and related services?

Answer: No. Section 300.226(a) states that EIS is " ... for students in kindergarten through grade 12 (with a particular emphasis on students in kindergarten through grade three) who are not currently identified as needing special education or related services, but who need additional academic and behavioral support to succeed in a general education environment."

Question B-5: What is the relationship between EIS funds and maintenance of effort (MOE) funds?

Answer: LEAs that seek to reduce their local maintenance of effort in accordance with 34 CFR §300.205(d) and use some of their Part B funds for early intervening services under 34 CFR §300.226 must do so with caution because the local maintenance of effort reduction provision and the authority to use Part B funds for early intervening services are interconnected. The decisions that an LEA makes about the amount of funds it uses for one purpose affect the amount that it may use for the other. Appendix D of the Part B regulations [71 FR 46817] provides examples of how 34 CFR §300.205(d), regarding local maintenance of effort, and 34 CFR §300.226(a), regarding EIS funds, affect one another.

C. Evaluation and Eligibility Determinations

Question C-1: Must an LEA evaluate a child upon the request of the parent at any time during the RTI process? May a parent request an initial special education evaluation at any time during the RTI process?

Answer: If the LEA agrees with the parent that the child may be a child who is eligible for special education services, the LEA must evaluate the child. The Federal regulations at 34 CFR §300.301(b) allow a parent to request an evaluation at any time. If an LEA declines the parent's request for an evaluation, the LEA must issue a prior written notice as required under 34 CFR §300.503(a)(2) which states, "written notice that meets the requirements of paragraph (b) of this section must be given to the parents of a child with a disability a reasonable time before the public agency refuses to initiate or change the identification, evaluation, or educational placement of the child or the provision of FAPE to the child." The parent can challenge this decision by requesting a due process hearing to resolve the dispute regarding the child's need for an evaluation.

Question C-2: May an LEA require that all children suspected of having a SLD first be assessed using an RTI process before an eligibility determination may be made?

Answer: If an LEA is using RTI for all its students, it may require the group established under 34 CFR §300.306(a)(1) and 34 CFR §300.308 for the purpose of determining the eligibility (eligibility group) of students suspected of having a SLD to review data from an RTI process in making an eligibility determination. Models based on RTI typically evaluate the child's response to instruction prior to the beginning of the evaluation time period described in 34 CFR §300.301(c)(1), and generally do not require as long a time to complete an evaluation because of the amount of information already collected on the child's achievement, including observation data. If the eligibility group determines that additional data are needed and cannot be obtained within the evaluation time period described in 34 CFR §300.301(c)(1), the parent and eligibility group can agree to an extension of the timeframe. However, as explained in Question C-1, parents can request an evaluation at any time, and the public agency must either obtain consent to evaluate and begin the evaluation, or, if the public agency declines the parent's request, issue a prior written notice as required by 34 CFR §300.503(a)(2).

Question C-3: Section 300.309(a)(2)(i) states that the eligibility group may determine that a child has a specific learning disability if "the child does not make sufficient progress to meet age or State-approved grade-level standards in one or more" identified areas. Section 300.309(a)(2)(ii) states that the group may determine that a child has a specific learning disability if "the child exhibits a pattern of strengths and weaknesses in performance, achievement, or both, relative to age, State-approved grade level standards, or intellectual development" that the group determines is relevant to making an eligibility determination. Please explain how these two criteria differ from one another.

Answer: Section 300.309(a)(2)(i) reflects the use of the criterion that the child has not made sufficient progress in at least one of the following areas when using response to intervention as an aspect of the SLD identification process: oral expression, listening comprehension, written expression, basic reading skills, reading comprehension, mathematics calculation, and mathematics problem solving. Alternatively, based on 34 CFR §300.309(a)(2)(ii), the group could consider variation in a child's performance, achievement, or both relative to age, State-approved grade-level standards, or intellectual development that is determined by the eligibility group to be relevant to identification of a SLD using appropriate assessments. Under this criterion, a pattern of strengths and weaknesses in performance, achievement, or both relative to age, State-approved grade-level standards or intellectual development would be part of the evidence that a child has a learning disability.

Question C-4: The regulations require an SEA to adopt criteria for determining if a child has a specific learning disability (34 CFR §300.307(a)). Does this preclude the SEA from mandating RTI as the sole criterion used to determine if a child has a specific learning disability? Must an LEA follow the State-developed criteria for determining if a child has a specific learning disability?

Answer: An SEA must include a variety of assessment tools and may not use any single measure or assessment as the sole criterion for determining whether a child is a child with a disability, as required under 34 CFR

§300.304(b). However, an SEA could require that data from an RTI process be used in the identification of all children with SLD.

An LEA must comply with the criteria adopted by their SEA regarding this requirement. The requirements at 34 CFR §300.307(a) require that a State adopt criteria for determining whether a child has a specific learning disability. The *Analysis of Comments and Changes* accompanying the final Part B regulations, page 46649, clarifies, "... the Department believes that eligibility criteria must be consistent across a State to avoid confusion among parents and school district personnel. The Department also believes that requiring LEAs to use State criteria for identifying children with disabilities is consistent with the State's responsibility under section 612(a)(3) of the Act to locate, identify, and evaluate all eligible children with disabilities in the State."

Question C-5: When implementing an evaluation process based on a child's response to scientific, research-based intervention, the regulations require that a "public agency must promptly request parental consent to evaluate a child (34 CFR §300.309(c))" if the "child has not made adequate progress after an appropriate period of time (34 CFR §300.309(c)(1))." Please define "promptly" and "adequate" in this context.

Answer: The Federal regulations under 34 CFR §300.309(c) require that if a child has not made adequate progress after an appropriate period of time, a referral for an evaluation must be made. However, the regulations do not specify a timeline for using RTI or define "adequate progress." As required in 34 CFR §300.301(c), an initial evaluation must be conducted within 60 days of receiving consent for an evaluation (or if the State establishes a timeframe within which the evaluation must be completed, within that timeframe). Models based on RTI typically evaluate a child's response to instruction prior to the onset of the 60-day period, and generally do not require as long a time to complete an evaluation because of the amount of data already collected on the child's achievement, including observation data. A State may choose to establish a specific timeline that would require an LEA to seek parental consent for an evaluation if a student has not made progress that the district deemed adequate.

We do not believe it is necessary to define the phrase "promptly" because the meaning will vary depending on the specific circumstances in each case. There may be legitimate reasons for varying timeframes for seeking parental consent to conduct an evaluation. However, the child find requirements in 34 CFR §300.111 and section 612(a)(3)(A) of the Act require that all children with disabilities in the State who are in need of special education and related services be identified, located, and evaluated. Therefore, it generally would not be acceptable for an LEA to wait several months to conduct an evaluation or to seek parental consent for an initial evaluation if the public agency suspects the child to be a child with a disability. If it is determined through the monitoring efforts of the Department or a State that there is a pattern or practice within a particular State or LEA of not conducting evaluations and making eligibility determinations in a timely manner, this could raise questions as to whether the State or LEA is in compliance with the Act.

Question C-6: May an eligibility determination be made using only information that was collected through an RTI process?

Answer: Section 300.304 (b) states that in conducting an evaluation, a public agency must use a variety of assessment tools and strategies to gather relevant functional, developmental, and academic information about the child, including information provided by the parent, that may assist in determining eligibility and not use any single measure or assessment as the sole criterion for determining whether a child is a child with a disability and for determining an appropriate educational program for the child.

The Department provided additional clarification regarding this issue in the *Analysis of Comments and Changes* section of the regulations, page 46648. This section states, "an RTI process does not replace the need for a comprehensive evaluation. A public agency must use a variety of data gathering tools and strategies even if an RTI process is used. The results of an RTI process may be one component of the information reviewed as part of the evaluation procedures required under 34 CFR §§300.304 and 300.305. As required in 34 CFR §300.304(b), consistent with section 614(b)(2) of the Act, an evaluation must include a variety of assessment tools and strategies and cannot rely on any single procedure as the sole criterion for determining eligibility for special education and related services."

D. 3-5 Year Olds

Question D-1: Why don't early intervening services apply to 3-5 year olds?

Answer: Section 300.226(a) tracks the statutory language in section 613(f)(1) of the Act, which states that early intervening services are for children in kindergarten through grade 12, with a particular emphasis on children in kindergarten through grade 3. Thus, LEAs may not use Part B funds to provide EIS to non-disabled preschool children.

E. Service Delivery Models

Question E-1: Is the use of RTI required or just permitted?

Answer: Section 300.307(a)(2)-(3) requires that a State's criteria for identification of specific learning disabilities:

- Must permit the use of a process based on the child's response to scientific, research-based intervention; and
- May permit the use of other alternative research-based procedures for determining whether a child has a specific learning disability.

Section 300.307(b) states that a public agency must use the State's criteria in identifying children with specific learning disabilities. Thus, the State's criteria must permit the use of RTI and may require its use, in addition to other assessment tools and strategies, for determining whether the child has a specific learning disability.

Question E-2: Does each LEA have to select either RTI or a discrepancy model to determine if a child is a child with a specific learning disability?

Answer: No. The State agency must adopt criteria regarding the determination of SLD eligibility.

An SEA must include a variety of assessment tools and may not use any single measure or assessment as the sole criterion for determining whether a child is a child with a disability, as required under 34 CFR §300.304(b). An LEA must comply with the criteria adopted by its SEA. Section 300.307(a) requires a State to adopt criteria for determining whether a child has a specific learning disability.

The *Analysis of Comments and Changes* section accompanying the Federal regulations, page 46649, clarifies, "... the Department believes that eligibility criteria must be consistent across a State to avoid confusion among parents and school district personnel. The Department also believes that requiring LEAs to use State criteria for identifying children with disabilities is consistent with the State's responsibility under section 612(a)(3) of the Act to locate, identify, and evaluate all eligible children with disabilities in the State. We believe this provides the Department with the authority to require a public agency to use its State's criteria in determining whether a child has an SLD, consistent with §§300.307 through 300.311."

Question E-3: What services can be defined as early intervening services? For example, are physical therapy, occupational therapy, and assistive technology considered early intervening services?

Answer: State and local officials are in the best position to make decisions regarding the provision of early intervening services, including the specific personnel to provide the services and the instructional materials and approaches to be used. Nothing in the Act or regulations prevents States and LEAs from including related services personnel in the development and delivery of educational and behavioral evaluations, services, and supports for teachers and other school staff to enable them to deliver coordinated, early intervening services.

F. General

Question F-1: Please define "significant disproportionality" in the context of EIS.

Answer: Each State has the discretion to define the term "significant disproportionality," in the context of EIS, for the LEAs and for the State in general. In identifying significant disproportionality, a State may determine how much disproportionality is significant. However, the State's definition of "significant" must be based only on a numerical analysis, and may not consider factors such as the extent to which an LEA's policies and procedures comply with the IDEA or the compliance history of an LEA. Establishing a national standard for significant disproportionality is not appropriate because there are multiple factors at the State level to consider in making such determinations. For example, States need to consider the population size, the size of individual LEAs, and composition of the State's population. States are in the best position to evaluate those factors. The Department has provided guidance to States on methods for assessing disproportionality. This guidance is found at: http://www.ideadata.org/docs/Disproportionality%20Technical%20Assist a nce%20Guide.pdf.

Question F-2: Will early intervening services data be reported in State Performance Plans (SPP) or Annual Performance Reports (APRs)?

Answer: No. Section 300.226 directs LEAs to report EIS data to their SEA. It is not a part of the information that an SEA must report to the Department in its SPP or APRs.

Question F-3: For discipline purposes, would a student's participation in an RTI process be considered a "basis of knowledge" under 34 CFR §300.534(b)?

Answer: Generally, no. Participation in an RTI process, in and of itself, would not appear to meet the "basis of knowledge" standards in 34 CFR §300.534. The standards for whether a public agency has a "basis of knowledge" are laid out in the Federal regulations at 34 CFR §300.534.

Question F-4: When an RTI model is implemented, can an incremental process be used to train individual schools so that over time the entire LEA is implementing the model or must all the schools in the entire LEA be trained simultaneously?

Answer: If the State or LEA requires the use of a process based on the child's response to scientific, research-based intervention, in identifying children with SLD, then all children suspected of having a SLD, in all schools in the LEA, would be required to be involved in the process. However, research indicates that implementation of any process, across any system, is most effective when accomplished systematically in an incremental manner over time. If the LEA chose to "scale up" the implementation of the RTI model gradually over time, as would be reasonable, the LEA could not use RTI for purposes of identifying children with SLD until RTI was fully implemented in the LEA. Therefore, it is unwise for a State to require the use of a process based on the child's response to scientific, research-based intervention before it has successfully scaled up implementation.

Question F-5: How might EIS funds be used to support a process determining whether a child has a specific learning disability and to address the needs of students who need additional academic and behavioral support to succeed in a general education environment?

Answer: If EIS funds are used to support a process to determine whether a child has a specific learning disability there are three interacting identification/instructional dynamics that need to be considered: (1) identification of learning disabilities; (2) early intervening services; and (3) response to intervention (RTI). While the Department does not subscribe to a particular RTI model, the core characteristics that underpin all RTI models are: (1) students receive high quality research-based instruction in their general education setting; (2) continuous monitoring of student performance; (3) all students are screened for academic and behavioral problems; and (4) multiple levels (tiers) of instruction that are progressively more intense, based on the student's response to instruction. For example, an RTI model with a three-tier continuum of school-wide support might include the following tiers and levels of support: (1) Tier one (Primary Intervention), for all students using high quality scientific research-based instruction in their general education setting. It would not be appropriate to use EIS funds for these activities since these students do not need additional academic and behavioral support to succeed in a general education environment. (2) Tier two (Secondary Intervention), for specialized small group instruction of students determined to be at risk for academic and behavioral problems. It would be appropriate to use EIS funds to support these activities. (3) Tier three (Tertiary Intervention) for specialized individualized instructional/behavioral support for students with intensive needs. EIS funds could not be used if these students were currently receiving special education or related services.

Question F-6: Should services supported with EIS funds be scientifically based?

Answer: The No Child Left Behind Act and IDEA call on educational practitioners to use scientifically based research to guide their decisions about which interventions to implement. IDEA states that in implementing coordinated early intervening services an LEA may carry out activities that include—

1) Professional development (which may be provided by entities other than LEAs) for teachers and other school staff to enable such personnel to deliver scientifically based academic and behavioral interventions, including scientifically based literacy instruction, and, where appropriate, instruction on the use of adaptive and instructional software; and
2) Educational and behavioral evaluations, services, and supports, including scientifically based literacy instruction.

INDEX

D

E

Q

R

S

T

U

V

W

Y